Living a Life in Balance

An Elemental Journey of Self-Discovery

Cael SpiritHawk

Schiffer Publishing Ltd

4880 Lower Valley Road • Atglen, PA 19310

Designed by Danielle D. Farmer
Cover Design by John Cheek
Type set in Adobe Garamond/Calibri/Futura

ISBN: 978-0-7643-4748-1
Printed in China

Schiffer Books are available at special discounts for bulk purchases for sales promotions or premiums. Special editions, including personalized covers, corporate imprints, and excerpts can be created in large quantities for special needs. For more information contact the publisher:

Published by Schiffer Publishing, Ltd.
4880 Lower Valley Road
Atglen, PA 19310
Phone: (610) 593-1777; Fax: (610) 593-2002
E-mail: Info@schifferbooks.com

For the largest selection of fine reference books on this and related subjects, please visit our website at **www.schifferbooks.com.**
We are always looking for people to write books on new and related subjects. If you have an idea for a book, please contact us at proposals@schifferbooks.com.

This book may be purchased from the publisher.
Please try your bookstore first.
You may write for a free catalog.

Cover Image: Woman Meditating On Beach In Peace © Angela Wayne. www.bigstockphoto.com
Illustrations and diagrams by Christa Hoeffler

Dedication

FOR MY WIFE LIZ*,
without whom this book would
never have become a reality.

Acknowledgments

Special Thanks:

A book like this one, which is based in the real-world practices of real people, is not something that can happen in a vacuum. The book you hold in your hands is the culmination of the understanding I have gathered through teaching this material in workshops and classes to hundreds of people over the course of years. There are far too many to name, but it's important to mention that I learned as much from them as they ever did from me. I would like to thank the people of the spiritual community of ShadowGrove, who were the first people I worked with on these ideas; I would also like to thank those who have attended my classes at Fertile Ground Gathering each year since 2008, for their insights, questions, ideas, and perspectives; this material is better for their input.

In particular, I would like to thank Christa Hoeffler for her diagrams and illustrations, Brett Zwerdling for his pre-publication input, Lisa Metlak for her extensive and meticulous work on the manuscript, the editorial staff at Schiffer Books for all of their hard work, and my wife Liz* for her assistance, support, and encouragement throughout the process.

Contents

Introduction

*A better understanding of the self,
stronger connections, success within so
balanced relationships,
a closer connection to the Divine*

Countless books have been written on the subject of personal empowerment in one form or another. These books seek to guide an individual on the path to any of a number of goals: a better understanding of the self, a stronger connection with a partner or family, greater success within society, a more balanced relationship with the natural world, or a closer connection to the Divine (by whatever name).

Books that focus on any one of these areas limit the success of the reader by their very nature because they place boundaries upon the reader's focus. For instance, they make statements such as: "In order to truly seek the Divine, you must set aside personal relationships," or "It is necessary to understand the self before one can build strong relationships with others." These books are merely treating symptoms (e.g., an unbalanced relationship with a partner) rather than addressing the underlying problem: that in order to have relationships—whether with the self, others, the Divine, or nature—that remain in balance, it is not sufficient to simply correct things when they go wrong. It is necessary to understand the fundamental nature of balanced relationships right from the start, so that all of one's relationships are based on a solid foundation.

In order to build such a foundation, one must seek to correct not the symptoms of imbalance within any given relationship, but the causes of imbalance within all of one's relationships. That may sound like a daunting task. In truth, it is not a task that one can accomplish by simply waving a wand and wishing it so, but it is achievable with the proper guidance. This book is one avenue to that goal.

FOR WHOM IS THIS BOOK INTENDED?

This book is for everyone who seeks balance: balance in his or her relationships with the self, with family, with the broader scope of society, with the natural world, and with the Divine. It does not require that you follow any particular spiritual or philosophical path, and it does not propose to elevate any one path over any other.

This book is for those who wish to understand the fundamental nature of balance in all of the relationships in life, so as to build and maintain those relationships in a healthy, stable, and sustainable way.

A BIT OF BACKGROUND...

Many of the premises in this book are based upon the existence of Divinity in some form or other. For the purpose of the journey that you, the reader, are about to undertake, the Divine can bear whatever name you choose to observe: God, Goddess, the Great Spirit of the Universe, the All...whatever name you use, think of that when this book refers to the Divine.

The ideas, methods, and techniques presented here are ones that I have developed and used over the course of more than twenty years. During that time, I have followed more than one spiritual path, but what I have discovered is that the foundational premises of what I do and how I do it still work, no matter what path I am walking and no matter what name I give to the Divine.

The ideas I offer here represent a way to accomplish the goal of understanding the ebb and flow of emotional, psychological, and spiritual energy that is the basis of all relationships. Note that these ideas are only a way, not *the* way; there are as many ways of reaching this type of understanding as there are people willing to search for and find the answers. I present to you the method that I have used, which has worked well for me and for my students, in the hopes that it will provide you with a starting point—a basis of ideas from which to explore on your own in order to find your *own* way.

If it happens that you discover a new method that works better for you, whether it is based upon or entirely different from the techniques I have offered, use it! If, on the other hand, you find that my method works for you, keep using it. The key here is not to find the way that is best for everyone (for no such way exists) but rather to find a way that works for *you* and helps *you* to reach a greater balance in your life.

This journey of discovery is a practical one, not an academic one; you cannot know if a technique presented here will work for you unless you actually try it. There are several meditative exercises throughout the book, and it is important that you perform each of them before proceeding beyond. A book is not an ideal medium for conveying a meditative process because reading requires that the mind be focused on the book rather than on the exercise at hand. For that reason, I recommend that you do one of two things: work with a partner and ask him or her to read the meditative exercise to you while you perform it, or download a pre-recorded version of the meditative exercise from the following URL:

http://www.CaelSpirithawk.com/LifeInBalance/

Because this is a process of growth and because some of the exercises here will be easier for you than others, I highly recommend that you keep a journal of your progress. Having such a journal is helpful on many levels:

- It gives you a history of your journey for future reference;

- It helps you to recognize in which areas of your practice you need further work in order to achieve greater success; and

- It provides you a reference point from which to compare your experiences with others who are practicing the same techniques.

It must be that words, ideas,
    and thoughts carry with them a different
form of energy, beyond the physical.

What is this "Energy" we're talking about?

Almost everyone is familiar with the broad concept of "energy" in a physical sense. In fact, many of the challenges modern society faces are related to energy in some form or other: fossil fuels to provide energy for transportation, illumination, and industry; green and other renewable energy sources; and nuclear energy. All of these can be condensed into the collective idea of "energy"—that is, the potential to effect change in the world.

However, physical energy is not the only thing that has that potential. An idea, a thought, and an emotion are all things that have the potential to change the world in profound ways. Consider the ideas of great speakers like Dr. Martin Luther King Jr. or Mahatma Gandhi. In a purely physical sense, their act of speaking made use of energy to move the air and thus create sound. The physical energy involved was less than the physical energy put out by a madman shouting on a street corner, yet their words resounded around the globe, shaping the thoughts and ideas of people across continents and changing the world. It must be that words, ideas, and thoughts carry with them a *different* form of energy, beyond the physical.

We will be discussing that energy in this book: the energy of the world beyond the physical, which has the potential to shape ideas, thoughts, and emotions.

At a recent class I taught on this subject, I asked the participants to define energy, and one young lady gave a response that was perhaps the most succinct and profound answer I have ever heard: "Energy is Divinity in motion."

Divinity in motion: the potential to reshape the way we connect to the world around us by changing the way we handle the flow of emotional, psychological, and spiritual energy between ourselves and others.

Foundation

There are many different ways of viewing the Divine. Each is a different way of attempting to understand that which is, by its nature, beyond our comprehension. Enough books have been written on the subject and enough wars have been fought over it that the interested student can immerse him- or herself in volume upon volume of philosophy, theology, and history for a lifetime and still only scratch the surface.

One thing that is common among all of those paths and religions, however, is the idea that there is a bit of the Divine in each of us. For those who follow the religions of the Book (Christianity, Judaism, and Islam), the belief is that humans are the children of God, made in His image, and thus carry that divine spark, known as the soul, within themselves. Those who follow a path of Nature-based belief often hold that the Divine is in all things and thus in each of us as well. The peoples of the Indian subcontinent commonly use "Namaste" as a form of greeting; the word comes from Sanskrit and means "the divine within me bows to the divine within you." For each path of belief, there is some concept or idea of Divinity within each person.

The little bit of the Divine that is present in each of us is what connects to the little bit of the Divine in others, and then Divinity flows along that connection. It is that movement of the Divine that is the Energy we seek to understand, enhance, and refine.

ENERGETIC BREATHING

The human brain is a remarkable thing; it is responsible for controlling all of the minutest details of our body's actions. In order to have the capacity to manage all of that activity, the brain makes a few compromises: it takes shortcuts when it can.

An example of this is something that every single person in the world (except for a few who are physically incapable) does thousands of times each day: blinking the eyes. There is no specific physiological reason why the eyelids must be closed and opened in unison, and if necessary, a person can close one eye while leaving the other open. They are two completely independent actions for which the brain has created a shortcut. Closing only one eye is so rare that it actually takes *more* effort—a conscious act of will—to do it, whereas blinking both eyes together is something so automatic that most people do not even realize they're doing it at all.

With the idea of blinking simultaneously versus closing one eye at a time as a simple demonstration of the brain's tendency to use shortcuts and our ability to consciously override them, it is now possible to consider another of the brain's shortcuts, which combines two distinct actions that the body performs so regularly and so often together that it takes conscious effort to separate the two: breathing.

When we breathe, we are exchanging air with the environment around us. We take oxygenated air into our bodies, and we release air that is depleted of oxygen and rich in carbon dioxide. However, we are doing more than that: when we breathe, we are also moving energy into and out of ourselves.

For example, consider what you do right before stepping on stage for a big performance or before taking a big risk: you take a deep breath. Then, when the performance is done or the crisis has passed, you release a sigh of relief.

It's not just air you're breathing when you do this. In preparation for a psychologically challenging activity, you breathe in deeply in order to supplement the store of that Divine energy within you. That energy helps you to accomplish whatever it is that you are setting out to do. Then, when your work is done and you have no need of the extra, you release that energy back into the world with a heavy breath.

Recognizing the concept of "energy breathing" is the first step in Personal Energy Work. When we breathe, we are taking in and releasing energy as well as air. More importantly, the knowledge that we can consciously separate the flow of energy from the flow of air is the basis upon which all of the following concepts in this book are based.

EXERCISE 1: Conscious Energy Breathing

- *Arrange your body in a comfortable position and in a place where external distractions are minimal. Remove any restrictive jewelry and make sure that your clothing is comfortably loose. Close your eyes and begin breathing deeply. Breathe with your belly so that your shoulders and rib cage are relaxed. Breathe deeply and slowly, becoming aware of the flow of air into your body and back out again.*

- *For a count of ten breaths, concentrate only on the flow of air in and out.*

- *Continue breathing deeply. Become aware that with each indrawn breath, you are taking energy into yourself, and with each breath you release, the energy is flowing out of you, back into the universe.*

As you become aware of this flow, pay careful attention to it and ask yourself the following things:

- *Where does the energy go inside me when I take it in?*

- *What does that place feel like when the energy fills it?*

- *What does that place feel like when the energy flows back out?*

- *What does the energy itself feel like? Is it warm or cold? Does it have a color? A scent? Perhaps even a flavor or a sound?*

- *Keep breathing and observing the energy for as long as necessary for you to become familiar with the feeling and for you to become comfortable with the ebb and flow.*

Once you are familiar with the sensation of the energy entering and leaving your body, return to normal breathing, open your eyes, and take a moment to write down your experience in your journal.

After completing this exercise, you have taken the first step toward conscious control over the flow of energy that affects your body and, thus, your mind every day.

Do not be too hasty to move on from this exercise; you are in the process of changing the pathways in your mind through which your thoughts habitually travel. Each time you perform this exercise, you will be reinforcing the pathways of this new way of looking at the flow of energy. Perform the Conscious Energy Breathing exercise several times, on different days and at different times of the day, in order to familiarize yourself with the differences in energy flows that occur under different circumstances.

I recommend that you maintain a journal of your experiences for a couple of reasons. First, maintaining a journal will give you the opportunity to look back at your journey along this path and to see the progress you have made. Second, the very act of journaling forces us to take our unordered and abstract thoughts about a subject and refine them into something more ordered and concrete. Writing down your experiences with each of these exercises will help you to better retain what you have learned.

CENTERING

Now that you have become consciously aware of the flow of energy that occurs when you breathe, what is the next step? The next step is to use that awareness to deliberately *separate* the breathing of energy from the breathing of air to collect that energy in one place for later use.

EXERCISE 2: Centering

As with the Energy Breathing exercise, arrange your body in a comfortable position, close your eyes, and begin breathing deeply. Become aware of the flow of energy into and out of your body with each breath.

Once you are comfortable with this flow and aware of the place within you where the energy goes, take the next step: as you breathe in, allow the energy to flow into that place inside you, but as you breathe out, hold that energy in that place and simply release the air from your lungs.

This is similar in concept to blowing up a large balloon: to do so, you must exhale into the balloon then pinch the neck of the balloon closed so that no air escapes while you draw another breath. Retaining the energy within you is the same but in the opposite direction; as you breathe in, your notional "balloon" of energy fills up a bit, and you must mentally "pinch" it to hold the energy in while you exhale.

Repeat the process a second time: breathe in, allowing the energy to flow into you and collect in the same place as the energy from the previous breath. Then, as you breathe out, hold that energy in place and simply release the air from your lungs.

Repeat the process one more time: breathe in and collect the energy as it flows into you and then release only the air as you breathe out.

Now return to your normal breathing pattern: with each indrawn breath, allow energy to flow into you, and with each exhalation, allow the same amount to flow back out. Hold within you the reserve of energy you collected over the space of three breaths and observe it: how is it different from the energy you normally carry within you? Pay attention to where in your body it has collected and how that place feels now that there is so much energy gathered there.

Continue breathing normally, holding the reserve of energy in place until you have had time to become familiar with it.

Once you are used to the way the energy feels, reverse the process that you used to collect it: over the course of three breaths, draw in only air when you breathe in and do not allow additional energy to collect within you. Then, as you exhale, allow some of the energy you have collected to dissipate.

⬛ *After three breaths, your body's energy level should be back to its usual level, and you can return to breathing normally. Maintain this normal breath for a time, and when you are ready, open your eyes. Take a moment to write about your experience in your journal.*

Congratulations! Once you have completed this exercise, you have successfully and consciously manipulated your own flow of personal energy. Having done that, you have passed the largest hurdle; everything that follows hereafter is merely an expansion upon this basic concept.

If your success was limited with this exercise, try it again at a later time. Keep practicing it, no matter how successful you have been, and you will find that over time you have a much easier time manipulating your personal flow of energy.

One of my students recently asked me, "What if I can't completely separate the flow of energy when I breathe? Does that mean I've failed?" No, it does not. It is not necessary for the flows of energy and air to be totally separate; the fact that you are able to separate them at all, so as to collect some energy and hold it within you, is the entire point of the exercise. If you have done that, then you have succeeded and ventured into a new realm: the realm of conscious and deliberate control over the energy flows of your own body.

Now, recall the place within you that the energy collected as you performed the exercise. It does not matter where in your body the energy collects, only that you are aware of where that place is. Some people find that the energy collects in a ball behind their navel or Solar Plexus. Some feel it coalesce in their forehead in a place called the "third eye." Others find that the energy suffuses their entire body, creating a second "light body" that fills their physical body. People who are studied in the concept of the Chakras (energy centers within the body, as understood in Hindu practice) may find that the energy collects in their dominant Chakra.

Once you have identified that place within you where the energy collects, remember it. That place is called your Center. It is the place from where you perceive your own personal power emanating. It is, in a way, your energetic "home base"—a place within you that you consider most strongly *yours*. Subconsciously, when you begin to collect energy, your mind directs that energy to your Center because it is from there that the energy can be directed elsewhere at need.

Keep note in your journal where your Center is. It can and probably will change in location over time as your personal and energetic needs change. Tracking these changes in your journal can provide you with a handy tool for mapping these shifts within your personal, psychological, or emotional needs for energetic support. We will return to explore this phenomenon later on in the book.

Collecting energy in your Center is a simple yet very profound thing: it is an affirmation of self and, more importantly, of will. Only a being possessed of free will, and the freedom to exercise that will, can consciously direct the flows of energy. By actually doing it, you are making a statement to the universe; you are telling the universe, "I *am*." You are affirming not only your existence but your identity and your intention to assert that identity henceforth.

Those with a background in theology may recognize the words "I am" as God's statement of enduring presence in the Bible; it is no less a statement of enduring presence when we speak it. By declaring our presence, our identity, our *will*, we are doing something even more critical than affirming ourselves to the universe: we are affirming ourselves to ourselves. We are taking conscious control of that within each of us that is part of the Divine; we are giving ourselves permission to be who we are.

In modern society, we have a tendency to identify ourselves in particular roles: job, family position, religion, even sports-team affiliation, or musical preference. When we apply these labels to ourselves or allow others to apply labels to us, we are giving up that which makes each of us unique: the divine spark within. You may be a married female Buddhist who likes Sitar music. But "married female Buddhist Sitar fan" only encompasses those few things to which the labels apply. They don't account for your dreams or for the poetry that you write in your journal or for the fact that you stop your car in traffic to rescue turtles crossing the road... in short, the labels by which we often define ourselves fail utterly to capture the true essence of self that makes each of us unique.

When we take energy into ourselves, when we collect it in our Center, when we make the affirmation "I am" before the face of the infinite universe, we are not limiting ourselves to the labels of society; we are rejecting labels and instead embracing that each and every one of us is a unique part of a complex whole—a divine being among countless other divine beings, important not because of what we have in common but because of how we are different.

As each new person speaks, whether aloud or in silence, the words "I am" before the universe, and as each person takes up the power that was already within, labels become meaningless, and the meaning of the word "Namaste" becomes clear: "The divine being that I am greets the divine being that you are."

GROUNDING

As children, many of us were taught not to stand under a tree in an open field during a thunderstorm; the grasses of the field do not fear the lightning because none of the stems reach higher than any of the other stems. The tree stands taller than the grass, so if lightning is to strike, it is the tree that will be the target. Consider that lightning comes only once in a while, yet people walk all over the grass every day, and if enough people walk on it, they crush it into the soil.

By making the affirmation of self and identity and will—by Centering—we have to some extent made ourselves like the tree in the field. Before, we were of a type with everyone else: stems of grass reaching for the sky but still among the other stems and still easy to tread upon and knock down. By reaching higher and declaring our uniqueness, we have caused the universe and all those spirits that live within it to take notice of us.

There are things in the universe that are larger and more powerful than we are, as the lightning storm is larger and more powerful than the tree. There are sources and flows of energy that are far bigger than any one person can contain—the outrage of a mob, for instance, or the fervor of a political or religious rally—these are things that are overwhelming to many people. Yet, some people seem to be able to handle that much energy without flinching; people who stand before the crowd and *guide* the flow, to be as a tree that not only bears but seeks the lightning strike and yet suffers no damage. How do those people differ from the rest?

Is it that these people have a greater capacity to store and direct energy? That's unlikely the case; with rare exception, the physiological and psychological stresses that humans are able to tolerate generally fall within some predictable bounds.

If these people are unable to store and direct more energy than everyone else, how is it that they can handle such massive flows of emotional, spiritual, or psychological power? The energy is there, generated by the crowd. It must go somewhere.

If we visualize a person as a small cup and the person's capacity for handling energy as being the volume of that cup, we can perform some further visualization in order to understand what might be happening.

Suppose that, in its normal state, the cup is only one-quarter full of water. If we try to pour a gallon of water into that cup, it will quickly fill up, and the water will spill all around and make a terrible mess. This is not unlike what happens when we find ourselves in the midst of an energy-flow we are not prepared to handle: we take it for as long as we can, but eventually, we overflow and can handle no more.

Now, what would happen if there were a small tube or hose running from the bottom of that cup into the bottom of, perhaps, a five-gallon bucket? As we pour water into the cup, some of the water would travel through the hose and into the bucket. As long as we don't pour faster than the water can travel across the hose, the cup will not overflow...that is, until the larger vessel was full as well.

So instead of a five-gallon bucket, we might visualize connecting the cup to an even larger vessel, such as a swimming pool or a pond. Then, we could pour quite a lot of water into the cup indeed and not cause it to overflow. Those people who can stand in the surge of energy created by a crowd and guide it, direct it, and incite it to greater power—those people have a connection like this one: to a place with greater energy capacity than they have. They may or may not be consciously aware of their connection, but it is present; it's what gives them the ability to captivate and direct the minds of thousands.

One interesting thing about energy in all its forms is that it seeks to be in balance; if you place a hot thing and a cold thing into an enclosed space, eventually the heat between them will even out so that they are both the same temperature. A similar effect can be observed if we take our imaginary cup and lower it so that the water level of the larger vessel to which it's connected is between the bottom and top of the cup. When we do that, the water in the vessel and the cup will equalize so the level is the same in each. Then, if we pour more water into the cup, the water will re-equalize with the levels of both being slightly higher. Here is the really interesting thing: if we scoop some water *out* of the cup, more water flows back across the connection so the level between the cup and the larger vessel remains equal!

What can we take away from all of this? If we, as limited beings, have only a particular capacity to store energy, but could somehow connect ourselves to a larger vessel that has much greater capacity, then when we had to absorb more energy than we could normally handle, the excess would shift across that connection so our own level would remain steady. In that way, we can cope with large surges of energy from outside. Further—and more importantly—once we have established that connection, *if we are forced to spend energy, more energy will flow across that connection to keep our own level stable.*

This is a profoundly useful realization. No longer is our capacity to absorb energy from others or to offer them the energy they require limited by our own internal capacity! We can take whatever people give us and not be overwhelmed, and we can give people whatever they need and not be drained ourselves.

If we return one last time to the analogy of the cup and connect it to the ocean itself instead of to a limited vessel like a pool, its ability to maintain equilibrium, no matter how much water we add or remove, becomes as boundless as the ocean itself.

The act of making a connection between us (or, more precisely, our energetic Center) and something with boundless capacity for energy is commonly called *Grounding*.

EXERCISE 3: Grounding

As with the Centering exercise, arrange your body in a comfortable position, close your eyes, and begin breathing deeply. Become aware of the flow of energy into and out of your body with each breath. As before, over the space of three breaths, take control of the flow of energy and separate that flow from the flow of air into and out of your body. Collect the energy from three indrawn breaths in your Center and then return to the normal ebb and flow of energy as you continue breathing.

Once you have found and filled your Center with this collected energy, seek with your mind a stable place in the earth below you. That place may be right beneath you, just under the surface, or it may be quite a way down, where soil turns to bedrock. It does not matter where the place is, only that you reach out and find it with your mind.

Once you have found this stable place, this Grounding point, reach out from your energetic Center toward that point. You might visualize yourself as having roots that sink into the earth, seeking that place, or you might see yourself as a pillar of stone connected to the bedrock itself. How you choose to visualize the connection is not important; the only important thing is that you make that connection between yourself, your energetic Center, and the stable place in the earth.

Once you have established that connection, allow yourself to become aware of the ebb and flow of energy across that connection: from you into the earth and from the earth back into you. As you continue to breathe, pull energy across the connection into your Center.

Does this new energy feel different from the energy that was already stored in your Center? Is it warmer? Cooler? Does it have a different color or texture or smell? Become familiar with the feel of this new kind of energy; it is stable, boundless, and calm.

For the space of several breaths, allow energy to flow between you and the stable place in the earth.

- *Is there anything inside you, energetically-speaking, that you would rather not continue to hold on to? Do you have lingering stress from work? Perhaps something someone did to you today that hurt your feelings? Find something negative within you, and as you exhale, allow that thing to flow across the connection into the earth and be absorbed. Breathe back in, pulling clean energy across the connection to replace what you have just sent. Find another negative thing, if you like, and send that into the earth as well.*

- *Once you are familiar with the feel of the stable place in the earth, the feel of your connection to it, and the feel of the energy that comes from it, allow yourself to release the connection and return to your energetic Center. Then, over the course of a few breaths, release the energy that remains stored there.*

- *Return to normal breathing for a time, and when you are ready, open your eyes.*

- *Take the time to think through what you have just felt, and write down everything you can remember in your journal.*

Just as Centering is a very profound step to take, Grounding consciously for the first time is a watershed moment. People who have an instinctive ability to cope with large flows of energy, such as those generated by emotional crowds, often have an instinctive ability to ground, and it is in that way that they are able to stand in the flow and not be overwhelmed. However, the problem with instinctive Grounding is that, because it is not under our control, we cannot rely on it to adapt to new situations as they arise, and we cannot be sure that our instinct will always ground us when we need it.

By taking deliberate and conscious control over our ability to ground, we ensure that we are able to adapt our connection to the earth to the needs of the moment, either by making it wider with greater capacity if we know that we will be dealing with a massive surge, or by making the connection in advance so that we can draw energy across it when an unanticipated need arises.

Centering is a declaration to the universe and the self; so is Grounding. When we Ground, we are affirming that "I am *here*." That is to say, "I am in a stable place and will not be moved by the flows of energy around me." It is the equivalent of erecting a lightning rod on that tree in the middle of the field; anything that strikes it will be shunted harmlessly into the earth.

I have heard of other teachers who teach these two activities, Centering and Grounding, in the opposite order from how they are presented here. In fact, the phrase "Ground and Center" is a common one in energy-work circles, and for that reason, many people assume that the Grounding should come first.

I reject that notion and present the order as I have here, because it is necessary for us to be Centered, to have the deep, intimate, visceral understanding of *self*, of identity, in order for Grounding to have any meaning at all. Why, as an example, would we tie a dog to a stake in our yard, unless we were sure that it was our dog?

SHIELDING

We have made an unequivocal affirmation of identity ("I am") by Centering. We have built upon that by making an equally-definite affirmation of stability ("I am *here*") by Grounding. However, it is not enough to know and declare who we are, nor even to know and declare who and where we are. Consider that a man who is tied to a piling at the end of a pier, staring at an oncoming hurricane, may know who he is, and he certainly knows where he is, but that does not mean that he is safe from the coming winds. Though the storm cannot move him from his place and cannot take his identity from him, it can still batter him with its power, for he has nothing to place between himself and that power.

So in addition to our affirmations of self and of place, we need one more affirmation: an affirmation of safety.

In order to protect ourselves from the unwanted intrusions of energy from outside ourselves, we need to create a shield that separates us from those unwanted influences. Doing so requires that we expend energy, and keep expending energy, in order to maintain the protection. It is fortunate that we have learned how to connect ourselves to a boundless source of stable energy, otherwise we would soon be depleted and unprotected, which is how we are before we begin learning these techniques.

Creating a shield

There are many different possible visualizations that one might use in order to create such a shield: perhaps a brick wall that surrounds us or a circle of light that we cast about us.

In most cases, it is my belief that the visualization we choose to use for any particular kind of energy-work is unimportant; the only thing that matters is the fact that we *have* a visualization that helps us to focus our will in order to accomplish the task at hand. However, when it comes to shielding, I depart from that philosophy for a particular reason: when we create a shield, we are defining a space inside where we can be safe. On the inside of the shield, there must be nothing that threatens that safety. Outside that shield, the energy flows of the world continue uninterrupted. The shield itself is a construct of mind and of will, which is nonetheless very real and which defines the boundary between these two spaces.

That is a critical concept, and one that bears repeating: the shield is a construct of mind. It is an embodiment of our will to be safe and protected.

Do not take that as a dismissal of the shield's power but rather the opposite; the energy flows that we are talking about are things that exist in the realm of the mind and that can only affect other minds. As such, the fact that the shield we create is something we create with our minds by focusing our intention means that there is *nothing* in the realm of these energy flows that can penetrate our shields and bring harm to us, as long as we know that to be so.

So we now have two criteria for a shield: We must *know* that it will protect us from unwanted outside influences, and we must ensure that, when we put it in place, there are no unwanted influences already inside it with us.

It's the first reason that causes me to reject the "brick wall" type of visualization; a wall can only go so far down and so far up, and that leaves openings above us and below us where outside influences can creep in. Because the shield is a concept—an *idea* of protection—if we allow ourselves to believe that the shield has weaknesses, then the shield will have weaknesses.

The second reason, the need to ensure that nothing unwanted is already inside our shield, causes me to reject any visualization that involves drawing a circle or perimeter around ourselves. If we wish to protect a garden from rabbits, there is no use in building a fence around it unless we can be absolutely sure there are no rabbits already in there, which will be trapped inside when we complete the fence.

EXERCISE 4: Shielding

> As with the Centering exercise, arrange your body in a comfortable position, close your eyes, and begin breathing deeply. Become aware of

the flow of energy into and out of your body with each breath. As before, over the space of three breaths, take control of the flow of energy, and separate that flow from the flow of air into and out of your body. Collect the energy from three indrawn breaths in your Center, and then, as in the Grounding exercise, establish a connection between your energetic Center and the secure place in the earth.

- *Once that connection is in place, begin to draw and release energy across it. Once you are comfortable with the ebb and flow of that energy, it is time to create your shield.*

- *As you draw a breath in, pull energy across your Ground connection, into your energetic Center. But do not release it back across the connection when you exhale. Instead, as you breathe out, visualize that energy expanding from your energetic Center in a shell, pushing everything that is not "you" in front of it. Allow the shell to expand until it is large enough to completely surround you in a sphere of protected space.*

- *With your next indrawn breath, pull more energy across your Ground connection into your energetic Center, and then as you exhale, visualize a second shell of energy expanding from your Center to join the first.*

- *Repeat this process once more, so that a third shell of energy expands and joins the other two.*

- *Now take a moment to become aware of the feel of the space inside your newly-created shield. As the shells expanded, they pushed every unwanted bit of energy away from you, leaving you in a safe place. Explore the sensation of this safe place with your mind. Explore the feel of the shield from the inside. Look through the shield and see the world beyond, full of energy flows that cannot reach you unless you allow them to.*

- *Once you have become familiar with the feel of your shielded space, you may allow it to dissipate so that you can feel yourself reconnecting with the outside influences of the world.*

- *Release your connection to your Ground and then, as in prior exercises, let the energy stored in your Center return to the world over the space of three breaths.*

- *When you are done, open your eyes and take a moment to write about your experience in your journal.*

The exercise of shielding completes the affirmation of will that we began with the Centering. That Centering gave us the identity of "I am." The Grounding built stability upon that, giving us "I am here." Finally, the Shielding added security to that affirmation, giving us "I am safe here."

"*I am safe here*": a definitive statement that encompasses all of our needs when dealing with the flows of emotional, psychological, and spiritual energy.

MAINTAINING YOUR SHIELD

Over time, as external influences wear against your shield, you may perceive that it is weakening. If you find that this is the case, you can always reinforce it from the inside by simply drawing another breath's worth of energy across your Ground connection into your Center and then releasing it and allowing another shell of power to expand from your Center to join the already-present shield.

This is another useful aspect of this particular visualization: there is no limit to the number of layers that you may choose to add to the shield from the inside, so as external energy flows chip away at your protections, you can always add more layers and remain completely secure.

SHIELDING GOES BOTH WAYS

It may have occurred to you that there is a second use for shielding: if a shield can be constructed to keep unwanted external influences from reaching us, could that shield not also work in the opposite direction, by keeping things that we do not wish to share with the world from reaching others?

It absolutely can. There are many different reasons why we might want our shields to contain our own energy and not allow it to influence another. Perhaps we are fearful during an emergency, but we do not want that fear to affect a child we are helping. Perhaps we are at a wedding, but in a foul mood for whatever reason, and we do not wish for our negative emotions to get in the way of other people's joy. Or perhaps we have a surprise for our partner, but don't want our excitement to let him or her know that something is up.

The reasons are countless, but the answer remains the same: Your shield is *your* shield, and it answers to your will. If you do not wish for an external influence to reach you through the shield, then it cannot. Likewise, if you do not wish for an internal influence to reach the outside world through the shield, then it cannot.

SELECTIVE SHIELDING

We do not always wish to exclude all external influences, and so it may—in fact, it almost certainly *will*—become necessary to create a shield that is selective in what it keeps out and what it lets in.

When we have a life-partner, we usually do not want to block the energetic connection we share with that person. When we are counseling a friend, we might wish to allow that person's emotions to reach us, so that we have a better understanding of what they are going through (then again, if their emotions are destructive, we might want to block them out entirely). We might wish to allow some influences, such as love or joy, to reach us as a matter of course while only blocking out negative flows of energy.

It is entirely possible to construct your shield in order to accommodate these circumstances. Technically, it is not even necessary to do anything special in order to accomplish this. Since the shield is a construct of mind guided by will, it is what we choose it to be, always.

However, some people find it helpful to use shield visualizations that are analogous to the things they want to allow and to deny access.

The simplest of these visualizations is perhaps color. Take a moment to think about what colors represent certain feelings for you. Perhaps you might think of anger as being red and of joy as being blue or green. It does not matter if the colors that you choose are the same colors others might use. It is only important that the colors you use represent your own internal associations. If you wish to create a shield that protects you from anger and hate, but allows joy and love to enter freely, then you might visualize your shield as being made up of colored glass, and the color or colors you choose would be the ones you associate with the positive influences. Light of one color cannot pass through glass of a different color, so if your shield is blue, then that is a simple mnemonic way of disallowing the red currents of anger from reaching you.

There are countless different visualizations that you might use to accomplish the same thing. Every time I teach this technique in a class setting, I ask the students for ideas about what visualizations might work, and most times they come up with at least one that I had not thought of before.

Some of the more interesting selective-shielding techniques that students have mentioned are:

Texture: *Visualize the shield as having the same texture as a comfortable, fuzzy blanket, so that it only allows comfortable fuzzy influences through.*

Compatibility: *Visualize your shield as being made of water and think of negative influences as being oily; oil and water do not mix, so those influences cannot penetrate the watery shield.*

Temperature: *A shield that only permits warmer feelings to enter and blocks colder ones.*

Radio Frequency: *One student always felt as if computers and other electronics created energy that influenced her in a negative way. Another student, an engineer, pointed out that electronics all create radio-wave interference of some particular frequency, and if she visualized her shields as being "tuned to a different station," then the unwanted energy would be reflected away from her.*

Shape: *Many of us are familiar with the plastic child's toy that is a red-and-blue ball with differently-shaped holes in it, and the yellow plastic blocks that will only fit through holes of the same shape; if we visualize various types of energy as having certain shapes, we can then construct a shield with holes that only admit "properly-shaped" energy.*

These are only a few of the types of visualizations that people have shared with me over the years, but they provide a good idea of the broad range of visualizations that one might choose to use. Which visualization *you* use only matters insofar as it must be a visualization that works for you. Try several different ones. If one works well for you, continue using it and reject the ones that work less well or do not work for you at all.

A WORD ON THE SUBJECT OF GEOMETRY

Every time I teach a class on this subject, one of the students will invariably ask a question along the lines of: "If I build my shield as you suggest, as a sphere big enough to completely surround me, but I'm close to other people, won't they be inside my shields? Or if they have shields, too, won't mine and theirs collide?" One student in a recent class referred to this as the "dinner roll problem": several dinner rolls in a pan rise and expand until they touch one another, and then each is forced into a square shape in the pan.

If we were dealing with a purely physical shield, the answer would be "yes, this is a problem"; a six-foot-tall person needs a shield big enough to *contain* a six-foot-tall person, and if that shield is to be spherical, then that means a sphere at least six feet across. Put several such people in a room, and it would be like a box of hamsters in hamster-balls—a lot of thumping about and no one getting anywhere.

Fortunately, we are *not* dealing in the realm of the physical; we are dealing in the realm of the mind, and in the mind, our energetic constructs do not need to obey the laws of physics. It is entirely possible for a person to create a spherical shield that excludes the influences of even a person standing only a foot away. In the conceptual mind-space of energy-work, we can separate ourselves from others by any distance we choose so that there is plenty of room for our shields (and theirs, if applicable) between us.

The converse of that is: yes, it is entirely possible to *include* someone else within the space of our own shields; that way, there is nothing impeding the connection between us and that other person. We might choose to do this with a life partner, for instance, in whom we trust completely. It is also common for a healer to do this with a client, and in so doing, the healer not only provides freedom of connection between healer and client, but also allows the healer to protect the client from outside influences that the client may be incapable of filtering out on his or her own. This is possible regardless of proximity, because in our mind-space, we can be as close to that other person as we choose, and physical separation makes no difference.

If the idea of spherical shields that overlap without actually intruding upon one another is one that you cannot wrap your mind around, and the Dinner Roll Problem is one you cannot overcome, feel free to modify the Shielding visualization so that the shells you send out from your Center are more elliptical—tall enough to contain you, but narrow enough not to collide with the personal space of others.

BUILDING CONFIDENCE

It is often difficult for people new to energy work to accept the idea that protecting themselves from external influences is as simple as willing it and visualizing it, but it really is that simple. Note that I did not say *easy*; these techniques may take you some time to master and become comfortable doing. That's okay. If you have trouble with one of the exercises, just keep practicing it until it becomes easier.

In order to build confidence in the effectiveness of your shields, *use* them. Shield yourself and then go to a place where there are a lot of people, paying attention to the fact that you are separated from their influence. With each success, your confidence in your ability to shield yourself will grow, and as your confidence grows, your shield will become stronger and more secure.

MOVING FROM EXERCISE TO PRACTICE

The exercises that we have performed so far have offered a step-by-step process that we can follow to go from our default unprotected state into the "I am safe here" state of being Centered, Grounded, and Shielded.

These exercises can take a long time to go through; the full Shielding meditation, as written, can take several minutes, if we are not in a hurry and we pay careful attention to each step. However, there are times when we do not have the time available to go through all of the steps in such a deliberate way. There are two practical solutions to this problem. The first is to make the whole process of Centering, Grounding, and Shielding much faster. The second is to eliminate the need to suddenly do it, by doing it once each day and then maintaining that shielded state throughout the day. You might be tempted to take the "easy" route and skip straight to the "do it once" method. Don't. That method requires much more familiarity and comfort with the process than you will have until you have been practicing for a while, and the best way to get that practice is to use the "making the process much faster" method.

From this point forward, I'm going to refer to the whole process as "Shielding," but when I do so, understand that I am referring to the entire sequence of Centering, Grounding, and then Shielding.

SPEEDING UP THE PROCESS

As with all things that involve many steps, the best way to become faster at the Shielding process is to practice—and then practice some more.

It is specifically important that you do not try to go fast. The quote "Slow down, you'll go faster" has been attributed to many teachers in many disciplines, but it conveys a critical truth: when we *try* to go fast, we become concerned more with speed than with correctness, and so we make mistakes and end up wasting time correcting them. When we simply do what we know how to do at a speed that allows us to do it perfectly, then over time that speed will increase until we can perform what seems like an immensely complex set of steps in a very short time indeed. Sergeant Alvin York, a decorated hero of World War I, phrased it thus: "Slow is smooth, and smooth is fast."

Consider the first few times you undertook any relatively-complex process—for instance, preparing to drive a car. In the beginning, there were so many things to remember: get in, close the door, adjust the seat, adjust the mirrors, put on the seatbelt, put the key in the ignition, put your foot on the brake, press the clutch (if it's a manual), make sure the car is not in gear, turn the key, release the parking brake, check the mirrors for oncoming traffic, put the car in gear, and then go.

That's over a dozen steps. Some of them you might not need to perform every time, like adjusting the seat and mirrors if no one else has driven that car since you last did, but most of them remain necessary every single time you get behind the wheel. Once you've been driving for a year or two, you never even *think* about them; you've done them so many times that they have become subconscious habit.

What used to take you several seconds or a minute to do, every time you sat down in the car, now takes you a matter of moments—a mere breath or two. You probably do it so fast that an ignorant outside observer might not even realize all of the steps you have taken.

The same thing is true with the Shielding process. You begin with a list of things that you must do: close your eyes, breathe, separate the energy flow from the air flow, collect energy in your Center, reach out to find the stable place in the earth, connect your Center to it, draw energy across the Ground connection, release it to form a Shield shell, draw more, release another shell, draw more, and release a third shell, open your eyes. Just as with getting ready to drive, you have a process of more than a dozen steps to go through.

Some of these steps in Shielding can be omitted, just as with the "driving a car" process. Closing your eyes is helpful for excluding distractions while you are becoming familiar with the techniques, but it is not required for the process itself. If you find that you can concentrate fully on the process with your eyes open, you may omit that step. Likewise, once you are familiar with the feel of the stable place in the earth, there is no need to seek it and find it each time; you *know* where it is, so you can simply connect to it.

Practice the full process daily, at the very least, and several times during the day if possible. Over time, you will notice that, just as with the steps required to start the car, the steps required to go from unshielded to Shielded will seem to condense into an automatic process that takes less and less time.

"Breathe, Separate, Collect, Center, Seek, Ground, Pull, Breathe, Shell, Shell, Shell" will become:

"Breathe, Collect, Center, Ground, Pull, Shell, Shell, Shell," which will become:

"Breathe, Center, Ground, Pull, Shield," which will become:

"Center, Ground, Shield," which will become:

"Center/Ground/Shield," which will eventually distill down in your mind and practice into:

"Shield"—a single word and concept that will encompass all of the steps necessary to ensure that "I am safe here."

Once you have reached this level of proficiency with the process, you will be ready to handle even the most sudden and overwhelming bursts of energy; with a single breath, your mind takes all of the steps that you have learned and practiced (and practiced some more), and in the space of that breath, you have created around you a perimeter of protection from whatever arises.

MAKING "SHIELDED" YOUR DEFAULT STATE

The next question we must answer is: "why bother waiting until we suddenly need shields? Why not simply put them up and keep them up?" The short answer is: "There's *no* reason why not." The slightly-longer answer is: "The only thing keeping us from doing this is that we must have the process down so well that we do not have to think about it in order for our subconscious to maintain that Center, hold onto that Ground, and replenish those Shields, so our conscious mind is free to go about its other business." That's why in order to do this, one must first go through the practice necessary to make the process fast. (You did take the time to practice, instead of skipping ahead to this section, right?) Not because it needs to be fast in order to maintain it all day, but because the familiarity and comfort level required to maintain it all day are the same familiarity and comfort that come from learning to go through the process quickly.

Once you have reached that level of familiarity with the process, setting up your shields when you wake up and keeping them up throughout the day is a relatively simple process; all it takes is practice.

For the whole thing to work, you need to go through the Shielding process at the beginning of the day, or whenever you decide to begin, then simply allow your Shield to remain rather than dissipating, leave your Ground connection to the earth in place, and let your Center remain energized.

That's it—simple but, again, not necessarily *easy*. At first, if you stop paying attention to the Shield, it might tend to wisp away. If you do not check on the Ground connection, you might find that it has come undone. If you fail to keep your Center energized, all of the wheels come off the cart because it is the foundation upon which all the rest is based.

For that reason, the first few times you try this, you're going to have to keep "checking in" to make sure that all is as it should be; every few minutes, reaffirm that your Shield is still there, your Ground is connected, and your Center is well-established. If they are not, re-establish them. Set reminders for yourself or leave notes around the house to check periodically, if necessary. You might wish to do this on a day when you don't have a lot of other commitments, so that you can refocus yourself every few minutes to reinforce your energy work. Over time, as the reminders create a pattern in your mind, you will find that you do not need to consciously check as often because your subconscious will begin checking for you and performing any maintenance that is required. That's why we had to refine the process into one that we didn't need to think about—so that it could continue on while we're not thinking about it. It will have become just like blinking: a set of discrete actions that you are so used to performing together that you habitually perform them all at once without conscious thought.

Don't worry if at first you can't make it through a full day with your shields intact. If you can only do it for ten minutes one day and half an hour the next, that's still progress—and it's *good* progress. Keep at it, and soon half an hour will become two hours, and two will become six; before too many days, you will find that your shields have become reflexive and habitual, and you will wonder how it was that you got along all those years without a way to filter out all of the nonsense from outside.

Your need for shielding will vary during the day and also from day to day. Once you are used to having shields in place all the time, you will find yourself reinforcing them automatically when the need arises and letting them relax when you are able. You can consciously control this, but often it is not necessary; once you have trained your subconscious to maintain and adjust your shields, it becomes just as natural as breathing—it becomes a part of you.

CONSEQUENCES

Once this process of energy work has reached the point where it is as breathing and requires no specific conscious effort, you may find that it is having other effects on your life as well.

Having a Shield in place protects us from the unwanted emotional, psychological, and even spiritual intrusions of others, which in turn has a couple of effects. First, it makes us less fearful about interacting with others, especially groups, because we no longer are at risk of being swept away by the group's influence. Second, rather than forcing us to be more withdrawn from people as the idea of Shielding might imply, it actually allows us to become *closer* to people because we are no longer afraid of their negative emotions affecting us. As a result of these two changes, you may find that people see you as both more confident and more caring.

Having a constant connection to Ground provides us with a stability that we did not have before. It means that we can "roll with the punches" to a greater extent, because any excess energy that we do take in gets harmlessly shunted to the Ground. You may notice that, as a result, people begin to perceive you as a sort of "sheltered harbor," both as a resource for stability in their own times of need and also as an example of how they themselves can become more stable.

Having and maintaining an energized Center constantly reinforces our own unique and undeniable sense of self, of identity, and of purpose. Keeping your Center active throughout each day will help you to become more purposeful in your life, less easily distracted by irrelevancies, and more focused on your goals. Ultimately, this will lead to greater success in more or less everything you undertake.

As an added bonus, we can make use of our subconscious mind in order to maintain this entire energetic infrastructure while we go about our daily lives. However, in so doing, we are *training* our subconscious as well. When we sleep, our conscious mind goes on holiday, and the subconscious is given run of the house, so to speak. Once you have trained your subconscious to deal with various types of emotional, psychological, and spiritual energy, it will keep doing so, even while you are asleep. This may lead to better sleep with fewer interruptions—and fewer nightmares, as negative energy is shunted down your Ground connection into the earth.

If you have reached this point in the book by performing all of the exercises and taking the time to practice each of them several times until you have reached the point where you can maintain yourself in a Centered, Grounded, and Shielded state without conscious effort, you have reached the first plateau in the development of your own Personal Energy Work.

If you have not, I *strongly* recommend that you go back and do so before reading further. Really. I'll wait.

Okay. Now that everyone reading this is on an even footing and can perform the entire Shielding process at a subconscious and reflexive level, we can proceed.

The
Elements

...the ability to cope with and
endure vast surges of energy from
outside, and it offers us a boundless
resource of energy from which we
may draw in order to continue to protect
ourselves indefinitely.

An Elemental Framework

The process as described so far gives us the ability to cope with and endure vast surges of energy from outside, and it offers us a boundless resource of energy from which we may draw in order to continue to protect ourselves indefinitely.

However, that is all a very limiting view of the world. We do not want to shut ourselves *away* from the energetic flows; rather, we want to embrace them—to step into the dance of energy that is created and shared by everyone and everything that surrounds us.

Can we do that or must we always hunker down inside our shields and let the energy flow to the earth?

We *can*, in fact, step into a broader energetic world and take a more active role in the flow of energy between ourselves, our kin, society, nature, and the Divine itself. That is what all of this is about, after all: not only guarding ourselves against the negative but actively fostering and nurturing the positive, creating new connections with new people and shaping the relationships we have in a positive way through the use of consciously-directed energy.

What we have learned up until now is important—*critical*, in fact—not only for providing us with a way to protect ourselves from unwanted energy but also as a way of becoming intimately familiar with the techniques that we will be using as we explore the next level of energy work.

The techniques that we have learned so far will come back in future exercises. Keep practicing them. For now, we delve into theory.

The elemental model

The model that we will be using for our explorations into Personal Energy Work is the traditional alchemical model, which comprises four elements: Earth, Air, Fire, and Water. As you will discover later, I have modified this model somewhat for practical reasons, but we will begin with the unaltered model as a starting point.

WHY THIS MODEL AND NOT ANOTHER?

A model is a way of helping us to understand something that might otherwise be beyond our grasp. As such, a model is not a thing that defines something, but is a way of *looking* at something from a particular perspective. Depending on the quality of the model, it may provide a very effective way of looking at things, or a very poor one.

In order to be useful, a model must be sufficiently complex to explain the phenomenon we are attempting to understand, and it must also be simple enough for us to grasp. (If it is too complex, we would need a model *of* the model, in order to understand the model itself.)

The emotional, psychological, and spiritual energy that flows through the world is immensely varied and diverse; it has enough nuances, complexities, and interactions that we *could* probably apply a model as complex as the modern chemist's Periodic Table, which lists well over a hundred elements and still does not account for every detail.

However, such a model is not necessary for the everyday understanding and application of Personal Energy Work, any more than a detailed understanding of chemistry is required to operate a car. If most drivers' understanding of gasoline were that "it's a liquid with fire in it, and the car needs fire to go," people would still be able to get to work in the morning; the driver doesn't *need* to understand the underlying chemistry and physics in the way that the car's designers and mechanics do.

Elemental models to explain the observed phenomena of the world are common throughout historical cultures. Some models, such as the Chinese model, contain five physical elements whereas some, such as the model the Druidic clans of the Celts used, contain only three.

The four-element alchemical model is one that readily explains many physical—and therefore analogous energetic—phenomena, and it is one that is fairly familiar to people in Western society. It is for that reason that I have chosen to use it as a way of understanding and exploring further energy work.

AN EXAMPLE OF THE FOUR-ELEMENT MODEL
APPLIED TO OBSERVED PHENOMENA

When the ancient people looked at the world around them, they saw a few things as fundamental, ever-present, and unchanging in their nature: Earth, the foundation upon which all things live, walk, and grow; water, present in lakes, rivers, and oceans; and air, which surrounded them all the time. However, there was a strange thing: a bright ball in the sky, which gave heat and light. The only thing known to them that gave heat and light was fire. Fire was neither air nor earth nor water, so it must be a fourth element.

Given these four, people could explain the phenomena they observed around them. A tree, for instance, stood upon the earth and took elemental earth into itself, thus being imbued with the strength of stone. It drank up water with its roots, as well, and that water flowed as sap within the tree. The tree reached out into the air and took that in as well, collecting and storing the fire of the sun inside.

When a tree was cut and a log tossed into a fire, the fire that had been part of the tree escaped, the water that was in it bubbled out, and the air within wisped away as smoke. What was left was ash; the earthy remains of the tree.

That this model, this understanding of the growth cycle of the tree, is less complete than our own does not change the fact that it explained the process to a level sufficient to meet the psychological needs of the people at the time.

It is the same with this elemental model for energy work; it may not be as complete as some other model, but it explains the energetic interactions we'll be dealing with at a level that is sufficient to our needs.

THE TRADITIONAL ELEMENTAL DIAGRAM

Traditionally, the elements are conceived as existing as two pairs, each pair a balanced set of two elements that oppose one another: Earth and Air, Fire and Water. These pairs could be represented in a square diagram with the halves of each pair in opposite corners:

FIRE   AIR

EARTH   WATER

Some alchemists felt the need to further describe the elements according to their attributes and added axes for "dryness" and "heat" to the chart:

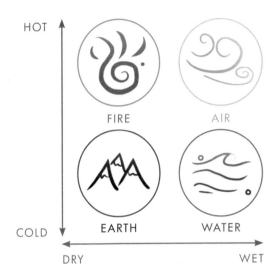

THE SPECTRUM OF VOLATILITY

However, if we dispense with the planar model of the elements for a moment and look only at a single attribute of each element, such as its propensity for change, we can arrange the four into a spectrum: Earth, the least volatile element, goes on the left end of the scale, followed by water then air and finally fire, the most volatile of the physical elements, on the right.

THE CYCLE OF WEATHER AND MIND

The human mind works well with analogy; analogies are simply another kind of model by which we can seek to understand something unfamiliar by comparing it with something that *is* familiar.

As the first step toward relating the elemental model of energy work to the human mind, let us first consider the elements in a familiar cycle: The Weather Cycle.

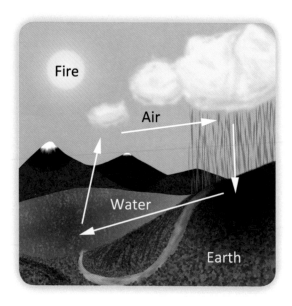

In this cycle, elemental Earth is the foundation; it provides the base upon which everything else occurs. It tends to resist change, so when Water flows across it, the Earth guides the Water into familiar channels. However, the Water *does* change the Earth, slowly over time, carving deeper valleys in the stone, moving river courses, and so forth. The Air picks the Water up from the ocean and drops it in distant places, whereupon the Water flows downhill back toward the sea. Driving this entire system is the power of the sun's Fire.

If we look closely at this system, we realize that each and every element is necessary to and part of the process. Without earth, the water would have no riverbeds in which to flow and no basins in which to collect. Without water, the face of the stony earth would never change. Without air to carry and move the water, there would be no water dropped in high places to then journey back to the low. Without the sun's fire to heat the water and cause it to evaporate and to heat the earth and air to create imbalances that cause the winds to move the evaporated water from place to place, the entire system would be static and dead.

Our consciousness has within it a similar process, and I refer to it as the Elemental Process of Mind. In this model of consciousness, Earth and Knowledge are analogous. Likewise, Water equates with Thought. Air is as the Imagination. Finally, Fire represents Inspiration.

Consider the weather cycle, with the labels replaced in accordance with this concept:

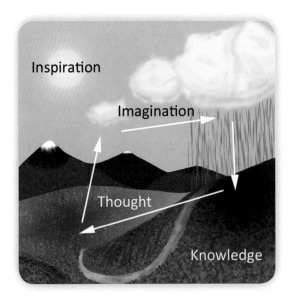

Like Earth, Knowledge forms the basis of our consciousness; it is resistant to change, because, after all, if we know something, what reason do we have to change it? As the valleys and canyons guide the flow of rivers, the shape of our Knowledge guides the direction of our Thought. However, as with Water and Earth, enough Thought can actually shape the underlying Knowledge; and once what we know has been shaped by what we think, our future thoughts tend to follow the new course, just as a river follows the bed it has carved. The Imagination picks up bits of Thought and drops them in places where they have never been before, and then that Thought explores the face of the Knowledge it finds there and is guided by it and shapes it in turn. It is Inspiration, though, that drives the whole machine, motivating the Imagination that carries the Thought that reshapes our Knowledge of the world.

Properties of the Elements

So now that we have the idea of an elemental model for energy work, we must determine how the model can actually apply to the energy work that we intend to perform. To do *that*, we must explore the attributes of the elements themselves so that we know what makes Earth "earthy" and what makes Fire "fiery." Once we understand and can describe the physical attributes of the physical elements, we are well on our way to understanding the elemental attributes of various types of energy. Once we understand the elemental attributes, we can then choose a particular type of elemental energy to use in accordance with whatever we need at the time.

EARTH

Earth is the foundation; it is the solid surface that lies beneath all other things in this world. It is stone and soil and clay and sand. It is the thing of which continents are made, the strong basin that holds the oceans, and the backbone of mountains that reach so far upwards that even the air is thin. From earth come the nutrients that nourish the crops and the trees. It is ageless and timeless, yet accommodates the needs of fleeting forms of life. It was here before humankind walked, before storms tore the atmosphere, before rivers flowed.

Earth is inert in that it does not seek to change its own shape and moves only when it is acted upon by some exterior force. A stone that is here today will be the same stone tomorrow. It is as it was, and it will remain so. When we refer to Elemental Earth, we are speaking of the archetype of this material; the perfect theoretical—or *ideal*—substance that embodies all of these qualities. Elemental Earth is the example of that which is permanent and enduring; that which is capable of absorbing and dissipating virtually limitless quantities of energy while remaining intact and unchanged. Elemental Earth represents the knowledge of the universe.

EXERCISE 5: Experiencing Earth

Most of us go about our lives without paying much attention to the Earth beneath our feet. To those concerned with the environment, "The Earth" is often more of a concept than an actual thing because we think about it in abstract terms rather than sitting down upon it and feeling it and knowing its magnitude. The following are several small exercises that you can do in order to become more familiar with the nature of physical earth. Some of them may not be possible for you because of where you live or because of some other limitation, and that's all right. Try as many of them as you can so that your experience is as broad as you can make it. If you cannot do some of them now, but may be able to later (for instance, if you live in a city but will travel to the country later on), remember to try the exercises when you can. It is never too late to add new experiences and new understanding to our way of looking at the world.

1. *Go outside into your yard or to some other outdoor place where you can be safe and undisturbed for several minutes. A park is a good place to go if you don't have a yard or garden of your own. Lie down on the ground in whatever spot seems right to you. Close your eyes and spread your arms and legs out wide, so that as much of you as possible is in contact with the earth. While you are doing this, pay careful attention to how the ground feels beneath you, how it supports your body, unmoving. Notice how no matter what is going on around you, the earth beneath you remains stable. Repeat this exercise, perhaps on different days, on as many different types of natural ground surface as you can. Try to include places that are not comfortable to lie on, as well, as a way of reminding yourself that the unyielding strength of Earth can be a detriment as well as an advantage.*

2. *Visit a cave, a canyon, a mountain, or some other natural formation of stone. As you stand before, beneath, or within the place you have chosen, contemplate the millions of years that the stone has been there, just as it is, and consider the time frame of an entire human life as compared to those millions of years. Realize that before every problem we face came into being, that stone was there before it, and for every solution we work out, that stone will be there, unmoving and unchanged.*

3. *Find a small stone that fits comfortably in your hand. Carry it with you throughout a day.*

4. *When you can, keep it in your hand and feel how over time it absorbs the heat from your body and then how it retains it for a while after you set it down. Even a small stone has a remarkable capacity to store heat. Experiment with this: allow the stone to sit in the sun for a while and then feel how long the stone remains warm to the touch. Note that through all of this transfer of energy, the stone itself remains unchanged. Remember this property of Elemental Earth.*

Each time you have completed one or more of these exercises, be sure to take the time to write what you have learned in your journal.

Now that we have a thorough experiential understanding of the nature of physical earth, we can take that understanding and use it to build an abstract idea of the archetype of Elemental Earth. It has several positive attributes; it is: strong, enduring, supportive, nurturing, stable, and sheltering. It has negative attributes as well; it can be: oppressive, unimaginative, inflexible, or burdensome. Look through the journal entries you have made while performing the Earth exercise set and see if you can add anything to the lists of positive and negative attributes of Earth, based on your own experiences and perceptions.

The archetype of Elemental Earth is all of the things on these lists. It is neither positive nor negative but has the potential for being either, depending upon the situation.

By applying these archetypal attributes of Earth to the concept of the energy that flows between people, we can begin to categorize some of the types of energy that are Earth Energy. On the positive side, we have: enduring strength of character, supportive and nurturing love, and a willingness to provide shelter and sustenance. On the negative side, we have: unwillingness to be open to new ideas, domination through force, lack of ambition or imagination, inflexibility and the inability to adapt to circumstance.

Take some time to think about what other forms of interpersonal energy, both positive and negative, might be categorized as Earth energy, and write them down in your journal.

WATER

Water is the element that moves across the earth, shaping and sculpting it. It is the fresh water of the river, the ice of the glacier, the salt water of the ocean. It is the basis for the blood that runs through our bodies. There is no part of the planet that lacks water; even in the most barren desert, there is water to be found if one knows where to look. It is essential to life as we understand it. Water seeks to be at rest and will travel great distances to find a low place, often moving with sufficient force to carve away even the hardest stone. Left alone, it will conform to the bottom of a container and will remain there for a time. Unlike Earth, Water is not inert; the water in a bowl will not flow up and over the edge to escape, but over time, the water will evaporate and be gone. Water is thus less constant than Earth. Where Earth is as it was yesterday and will be tomorrow, Water may be a river today, a cloud tomorrow, rain the next day, and a river once more the day after that. In all of those changes, its fundamental nature remains unchanged. When we speak of Elemental Water, we refer to archetypal Water: the conceptual substance that is fluid and accommodating enough to conform to the shape of even the most complex and delicate vessel but powerful and vigorous enough to cut channels and valleys through stone. Elemental Water is the model of that which is infinitely patient and adaptive yet forceful; that which changes at all times yet always remains the same. Elemental Water represents the thoughts of the universe.

EXERCISE 6: Experiencing Water

Water is something that we cannot live without, yet which we barely recognize on a daily basis. We use it and consume it without ever paying attention to its fundamental nature. The following are several small exercises that you can do in order to become more familiar with the nature of Water. As before, with the Earth exercises, you may not be able to do all of these right away—or at all. Try to do those you can and broaden your experience with the second of the stable elements.

1. *Find a small stream or brook and sit on its bank, observing the flow of the water. Pay attention to how chaotic, yet ordered, the path is that the water chooses to take as it travels downstream. Note that the Water seeks the lowest path, always, even if a shorter, faster path might be available if the Water were to simply go up and over a small lip of stone. Watch in faster-moving parts of the stream and see how sand and silt, tiny bits of Earth, are being carried downstream and how the Earth itself is being shaped by even this small flow. Look at the bank of the stream and see how far below the top of the bank the water's surface is. Consider how much earth the stream has already moved aside, one single grain at a time. Then consider a valley the size of the Grand Canyon and contemplate the sheer volume of stone that was cut away and removed by the Colorado River, in pieces the size of grains of sand or smaller. Imagine the perseverance of Elemental Water, the perfect form of this physical element that has brought about so much change on our world.*

2. *Visit the ocean and stand in the waves at the shore. Move into the water until you are at least waist deep and then attempt to stand immobile as the waves roll past you. Place a hand out in front of you with your fingers pointing straight ahead into an oncoming wave and your thumb upwards; feel how the water parts effortlessly around*

your fingers, palm, wrist, and arm, yet still carries sufficient force to move your body when it reaches you.

3 *Find a pool or pond—or the ocean on a calm day—and allow yourself to float on your back in the Water; feel how your body is enveloped with equal pressure from all directions. Note how there is no one part of you that is bearing more pressure than any other and how, after a few moments, there is no longer a sensation of pressure at all. The only place that you actually feel the Water is at places of transition, where the Water gives way to Air.*

Each time you have completed one or more of these exercises, be sure to take the time to write what you have learned in your journal.

We can take our experiential understanding of the nature of physical water and use it to build an abstract idea of the archetype of Elemental Water. It has several positive attributes; it is: powerful, supportive, flexible, life-supporting, persistent, and predictable in its behavior. Some of its negative attributes are that it can be: overly forceful, destructive, overbearing, and inconstant. Look through the journal entries you have made while performing the Water exercise set and see if you can add anything to the lists of positive and negative attributes of Water based on your own experiences and perceptions.

As with Earth, the archetype of Elemental Water is all of the things on these lists. It is neither positive nor negative but has the potential for being either, depending on the situation.

By applying these archetypal attributes of Water to the concept of the energy that flows between people, we can begin to categorize some of the types of energy that are Water Energy. On the positive side, we have: persistence and perseverance, flexibility, dynamic strength, gentle support, and the tendency to follow predictable paths. On the negative side, we have: overbearing persistence (such as nagging or henpecking), an unwillingness to stand firm when necessary, pushiness, and the potential to overwhelm and drown others.

Take some time to think about what other forms of interpersonal energy, both positive and negative, might be categorized as Water energy and write them down in your journal.

AIR

Air is the antithesis of Earth. Recall all of the properties of Earth, and you will find that Air is in opposition to them. Air is dynamic; it does not seek to remain as it is but expands to fill all available space. It is change, embodied; like the weather that is its outward sign, each day it can wear a different face. It has no great capacity to absorb and store energy but dissipates it through rapid movement. Air is the breeze, the wind, the gale, the hurricane. Its power is not in its own movement but in the movement that it can impart to other things. It is not in the nature of Air to impose its changing nature on other things; it adapts to the things around it, flowing above, beneath, and to either side. Air is a thing of avoidance, not confrontation. It lacks perseverance. Air is the reflection of imagination in the universe.

EXERCISE 7: Experiencing Air

Even more than Water, Air is ever-present, absolutely necessary, yet mostly unnoticed in our daily lives. The following exercises are designed to allow you to become more familiar with the nature of Air. As in previous exercise sets, if you cannot do all of these or must wait to do some of them, that's all right. But remember them and pay attention when the opportunity arises.

1. *Perform the observation exercise described for Water but use the smoke that rises above a bit of burning incense as your focus. As you concentrate upon the smoke, pay attention to the details of its movement. Make note of the fact that in some places it moves linearly, but before long it breaks down into swirls of chaotic complexity. See how moving your hand near the smoke can cause it to shift, even if you do not touch it. Place a finger or hand into the rising smoke and watch as the smoke moves around you, accommodating your presence yet continuing to move where it wills.*

2. *Sit beside a window on a sunny day. Position yourself so that you are not in the direct sun but are looking through the sunbeam from the side. It will help if you happen to have a place where you can do this that has a dark background, but it is not necessary. As you sit, watch the tiny motes*

and particles of dust as they move in the air and are illuminated by the sun. The particles themselves are not part of the Air, but they allow us to observe the movement of the air nonetheless. Pay attention to the fact that no matter how still the Air in the room seems to be, the dust (and thus the Air) continues to move, at least a little. Move your hand through the sunbeam and watch the dust motes swirl in its wake before eventually returning to their previous slow meandering. Consider the implications of this: The Air changed its state in order to accommodate the movement of your hand, and while that effect persisted for a few moments even after your hand was gone, it did not take very long at all for the Air to return to its prior state, as if you had never been there at all.

3. *Go outside on a breezy day and feel how the Air presses against your body. Pay attention to the fact that the pressure you feel is ever-changing; it pulses and shifts and varies from moment to moment. Realize how quickly the Air is moving, and yet how little "real" effect it is having on you. If you have performed the ocean-wave exercise for Water, consider the difference in force that even slowly moving water has in contrast to rapidly-moving Air.*

4. *On a breezy day, watch for swirls of dust or leaves. If you happen to live in a place where dust devils occur, go outside and watch for them—they're the same thing but on a larger scale. In an urban environment, the corners between buildings are a good place to look for the spiraling vortices of leaves and dust. Alternatively, go outside with a flashlight on a cool evening after a warm afternoon rain when there is mist rising from the road surfaces and watch for tall narrow columns of mist standing above the ground haze. All of these phenomena—the leaf swirls, dust devils, and mist sprites—are different manifestations of the same phenomenon. Ultimately, even larger systems, such as tornadoes and hurricanes, are no different in nature (only in scale) from these smaller vortices. Whichever of these you choose to observe, make note of as much as you can about it. Specifically, it is worth understanding the ordered nature of the swirl within the otherwise chaotic movement of the air. When the Air "gets organized," so to speak, it can have effects that are different from what we normally expect, and this is important to keep in mind. The leaves, dust, or moisture that is caught up in the column of spinning Air is contained, almost as if it were in a vessel of some sort, but when the vortex dissipates, it is released to fall where it may.*

As you complete these exercises, be sure to take the time to write what you have learned in your journal.

As with Earth and Water, we can take our experiential understanding of the nature of physical Air and use it to build an abstract idea of the archetype of Elemental Air. It has several positive attributes; it is: gentle, unobtrusive, very flexible, and refreshing. Some of its negative attributes are that it can be: flighty, ephemeral, unfocused, unreliable, and turbulent. Look through the journal entries you have made while performing the Air exercise set and see if you can add anything to the lists of positive and negative attributes of Air, based on your own experiences and perceptions.

As with Earth and Water, the archetype of Elemental Air is all of the things on these lists. It is neither positive nor negative but has the potential for being either, depending upon the situation.

By applying these archetypal attributes of Air to the concept of the energy that flows between people, we can begin to categorize some of the types of energy that are Air Energy. On the positive side, we have: gentleness, the flexibility to adapt to any situation, the ability to move in imaginative new directions, and the ability to flow around obstacles with little or no effort. On the negative side, we have: flightiness, unreliability, an inability to focus, a tendency to wander from the point, a lack of perseverance, and a lack of power.

Take some time to think about what other forms of interpersonal energy, both positive and negative, might be categorized as Air energy, and write them down in your journal.

FIRE

In some ways, Fire is not a physical Element at all. Some elemental systems, such as the Druidic, do not recognize Fire because it is intrinsically different from the three physical elements that we have discussed so far. Because the alchemists knew of only one source of heat and light that could be used by people and because they knew of only one source of heat and light in the heavens, they assumed that the Sun was a thing made of Fire, no different from any terrestrial Fire except in magnitude. They were partially correct, but they generalized in the wrong direction; rather than concluding that the Sun was made of Fire, it would be more correct to say that Sun and Fire are manifestations of the same thing: physical energy. When we think of Fire as a source of physical energy rather than as a substance, its relationship to the other Elements becomes clearer. Fire is the motivator. Fire is the thing that melts the stone and evaporates the Water and heats the

Air to cause the wind to blow. Though the nature of the other elements is intrinsic, it is the external influence of Fire that causes them to interact and reveal their properties. Fire is the source of heat, the source of light, the source of movement, of weather, of change. Fire is the embodiment of inspiration and emotion in the Universe.

EXERCISE 8: Experiencing Fire

Though Fire is not something that every person uses every day, it is the symbolic representation of physical energy, and that is something that everyone uses constantly. The following exercises are designed to allow you to understand the nature of Fire as a physical thing, as well as to understand the physical energy that it represents. Once again, do as many of these exercises as you are able to do *(and because some of them include the use of actual flame, remember safety in considering which of them you should do).*

1. *Perform the observation exercise as described for Air and Water, using a small candle as your focus. For the purposes of this exercise, the smaller the candle you use, the better: ideally, you should continue your meditation until the candle has burned out. As you meditate upon the flame, observe how it acts; note that, as with the Air exercises, you can cause the flame to move by moving your hand near it. See that as the flame burns, it consumes the candle; this is different from any of the other Elements with which we have worked. If you are able to continue the meditation until the candle burns out, do so; it helps to understand one of the intrinsic attributes of Fire: left unchecked, Fire will consume everything it can, and when its source of fuel is gone, so is the Fire, leaving nothing but waste.*

2. *Perform the observation exercise with a Fire in a fireplace or a small bonfire as your focus. Watch carefully as the flames dance across the wood; they change and move and shift with a rapidity that makes them seem almost alive. As with the previous exercise, note how the Fire consumes its fuel and leaves little behind. Feel the heat that comes from the Fire and understand that the heat you are feeling is the balancing gift that comes as a result of Fire's destructive nature. When you are done, ensure that the Fire you have built is safely extinguished. (Recall that, left unchecked, Fire will consume everything it can; you do not want your home or a forest or a park to be the thing on which the Fire feeds.)*

3. *Pick a sunny day with as few clouds as possible and find a secluded spot where you can lie down and feel the sun's rays warming you. It is a good*

idea to wear sunscreen when you do this because—just as with a bonfire—the beneficial effects of sunlight are balanced with detrimental effects as well. If you have a place to do this that is sufficiently private and safe, you may wish to wear less than your usual amount of clothing so more of your body surface can feel the effect of the sun. As you lie there, feel how the warmth of it seems to pass through you, not stopping at your skin. Recognize that the energy you are absorbing is the same energy that every other thing, living or not, absorbs every day.

4 *Go outside and observe the world around you. Note the movement of wind. If there is precipitation, make note of it. If you live near a stream or river, go and watch it flow. Recall all of the previous exercises that took you outside and remember all of the ways that the other elements moved and interacted. Realize that all of this motion, all of this interaction, all of this ongoing change relies on the external influence of physical energy as represented in our model by Elemental Fire. The wind blows because of Air, heated by the sun, rising and being replaced by cooler Air from elsewhere. Without the sun's Fire, there would be no wind. Rivers flow downstream from their sources, but the Water at the stream head came from rain evaporated from the oceans and transported by wind. Without the sun's Fire, there would be no rivers. Glaciers carve the very Earth they traverse, but the ice of the glacier came from the same clouds of evaporated ocean Water that formed the rivers. Without the sun's Fire, there would be no glaciers of ice. Volcanoes spew molten rock and ash from the center of our world, but the heat that melted that rock came from a time when the sun heated the dust that eventually coalesced into our planet. Without the sun's Fire, there would be no volcanoes. In short, without the energy that we symbolize as Fire, there would be no life.*

As you complete these exercises, be sure to take the time to write what you have learned in your journal.

As with all of the prior elements, we can take our experiential understanding of the nature of physical Fire and use it to build an abstract idea of the archetype of Elemental Fire. It has several positive attributes; it is: warm, energizing, transformative, inspirational, and illuminating. Some of its negative attributes are that it can be: all-consuming, destructive, and hard to control. Look through the journal entries you have made while performing the Fire exercise set and see if you can add anything to the lists of positive and negative attributes of Fire based on your own experiences and perceptions.

As with the other elements, the archetype of Elemental Fire is all of the things on these lists. It is neither positive nor negative but has the potential for being either, depending on the situation.

By applying these archetypal attributes of Fire to the concept of the energy that flows between people, we can begin to categorize some of the types of energy that are Fire Energy. On the positive side, we have: passion, invigoration, transformation, the inspiration of new ideas, the ability to burn away the unwanted old. On the negative side, we have: the potential for avarice, wanton destruction, consumption for the sake of consumption, the danger of hurting others, the potential for losing control.

Take some time to think about what other forms of interpersonal energy, both positive and negative, might be categorized as Fire energy and write them down in your journal.

MAKING USE OF THE ELEMENTS

Now that we have the archetypes, these *ideas* of what forms of interpersonal energy belong to which Element, we can begin to see how energy of different types can either be helpful or detrimental in any given situation.

The key is to evaluate a situation in terms of what elemental energy types are present in it, both positive and negative, and then to determine what types of energy we, ourselves, might bring to the situation in order to foster the positive and counter the negative so that the situation can be resolved in a positive way.

If we are dealing, for instance, with an extremely inflexible boss at work whose permission we need for something or other, what might we do? Extreme inflexibility is an attribute of Earth. In this case, it does not make sense to apply an Earth-energy solution to this problem, because it would be like two boulders crashing into one another. So if we refer back to the other elemental energy types, perhaps we can find a potential solution in one of them.

> *Water's attributes include persistence and perseverance. Recall the river that carves a canyon out of stone: it changes the earth, but it takes a very long time to do it. One strategy might be to carefully and slowly attempt to "carve the stone" of the boss' inflexibility by taking baby steps toward the ultimate solution; we might at first ask only for a small part of what we ultimately need and ask for more over time.*

> *Air's attributes include extreme flexibility and a tendency to go around, rather than through, obstacles. An Air-based strategy might be to see*

if there is another way entirely to secure permission. Perhaps there is a higher-up in the company who would encourage the boss to give permission, or perhaps there's a completely different way to accomplish the goal at hand—one that doesn't require the boss to sign off on it.

Fire is transformative. Perhaps the boss is unwilling to give permission because of something within her that makes her unwilling. A solution based on Fire might be to work in such a way as to help the boss transform herself from someone unwilling to give permission into someone who would give it willingly.

I will leave it as an exercise for the reader to determine which of these solutions—or another solution entirely—is the "best" one to use in the situation. It is my intention with this example only to show that, for any given problem, it's possible to break it down into the elemental forces at work and then select an elemental approach of our own in order to positively affect the outcome.

All right, so we now have a lot of theory and understanding of the nature of the physical elements and thus an abstract understanding of the archetypal energetic elements; that is one piece of the puzzle. Another piece that we hold is the ability to control the flows of energy into and out of ourselves. So how do we connect the two?

Before we answer that question, let's ask ourselves another: what do we do if we know that the correct thing for us to do at some given moment is to use the energetic properties of a certain Element, but we aren't feeling it, so to speak? We need that "Air" energy, but we just don't have it in us at that time. So do we just do without and not do what we know we should?

Or do we find a way to *get* the type of energy we need?

It turns out that we can get the energy of whatever type we need, when we need it, and the explanation of how to do that is the missing puzzle piece that connects the practical energy work we have already done with Centering, Grounding, and Shielding to the theory of archetypal elemental energies that we have recently come to understand.

Recall that when we Ground, we make a connection from our Center to the Earth, and we draw what we now understand is archetypal Earth energy through that Ground and into ourselves. That is all very well and good when the type of energy that we need is Earth energy. What if Earth energy is *not* what we need?

What if we require the perseverance of Water, the imaginativeness of Air, or the transformative passion of Fire?

Can we Ground, not in the Earth, but in one of these other elements?

LIMITED BY TERMINOLOGY

It turns out that yes, we can, indeed.

However, the term "Ground" is somewhat problematic in this situation; the term itself comes from the act of grounding an electrical circuit, which is accomplished by physically connecting that circuit into the soil of the Earth. So when we refer to Grounding, by definition we are referring to a connection to Earth.

Likewise, when we talk about establishing a conduit between our Center and one of the elements other than Earth, we will use the term "Connecting" rather than "Grounding."

CONNECTING TO THE ELEMENTS

You may be wondering what I mean by "connecting to an element." It is very easy to conceptualize a connection between ourselves and the Earth, because, after all, all we have to do is look down and there the Earth is ready for us to grasp.

Connecting to Air may be similarly easy to conceptualize, because—unless we're an astronaut or scuba diver—we're surrounded by Air constantly.

What about Water and Fire? How are we to conceptualize connecting to them? Most of us do not have an endless supply of Water or Fire lying about the house. Some live near an ocean, so they have that resource, but what of Fire? The sun is an embodiment of Fire, but there are times when it's not visible and available to us.

What are we to do? The answer to that lies in the fact that, when we are Connecting to an element, we are not making a connection between our physical selves and the *physical* embodiment of that element. If we were, we would need a physical conduit between it and us. Rather, we are using our minds to create a connection between our energetic Center and the archetypal embodiment, the idea of that element. That is to say, if we wish to Connect to Water, we can do that even in the most arid desert by Connecting to the concept of all of those things that Water is in our minds.

By doing this, a desert nomad can Connect to Water, and a diver can Connect to Air, and one who is alone in the dark can Connect to Fire, at any time, in any place. This is the realm of the mind, and in this realm, our only limitations are the limitations we place upon ourselves.

Before we begin exploring the ways of Connecting to the various elements, please note that there are hazards and risks associated with all of them except Earth; pay attention to the warning that precedes each exercise. I recommend that for *all* of these Connection exercises except Earth, you have a partner or "spotter" with you for the first few times you try it, in case the meditation takes you in a direction that you do not want and do not know how to reverse.

If you recall the Spectrum of Volatility, you will see that we are going to explore the elements in order of increasing volatility. As a rule of thumb, the more volatile an element is, the closer attention you must pay to it when you are working with it; more volatility means less stability, and that means less controllability.

EARTH

There is no need to perform a new exercise for Connecting with Earth; the exercise for doing so is one with which you are already familiar and have done many times: Grounding. When you need the type of energy that Earth provides, simply return to your Grounding exercise (**EXERCISE 3**).

WATER

You will remember that Water is adjacent to Earth on the spectrum: slightly less stable, but more stable than Air. It should therefore require a bit more care than

Earth but less care than Air does. However, because Water is much heavier than Air, it carries much more force when it moves than an equivalent amount of Air. For that reason, use caution when working with Water; if you slip, it can sweep you away before you notice.

EXERCISE 9: Connecting to Water

Remember as you proceed with this visualization that it is yours to control and yours to end if, at any time, you feel yourself beginning to lose control of the flow of energy.

- *Just like when you prepare to Ground, place yourself in a comfortable position, close your eyes, and begin breathing deeply and regularly. Become aware of the flow of energy into and out of your body with each breath. As before, over the space of three breaths, take control of the flow of energy and separate that flow from the flow of air into and out of your body. Collect the energy from three indrawn breaths in your Center and then return to the normal ebb and flow of energy as you continue breathing.*

- *Now form a picture in your mind of a place where there is Water. Depending on your own level of comfort, this may be a small thing, perhaps a pool or small, still pond. Or it may be a greater place, such as a vast lake or the ocean itself.*

- *The water in this place is calm. Not unmoving, for Water is never completely at rest but not forceful in its movement.*

- *You might picture yourself as standing at the edge of this place or in a small boat upon its surface, or, if you like, floating in it, gently supported by the Water. It is not important which one you visualize.*

- *Once you have this visualization firmly in mind, reach out from your energetic Center and form a connection with the Water in this place. It does not matter what form this connection takes, as long as it is the connection that feels right to you. You might envision a tendril of Water that reaches out from the surface and connects directly to your energetic Center. You might find yourself becoming as Water yourself and mingling with the Water in this place.*

- *Whatever way of connecting you wish to use, find it and know that the connection exists. Once you have done that, begin to draw energy across the connection. With each breath, take some of the energy of the Water into your Center.*

 How is this energy different from the energy of Earth? Is it warmer or cooler? Does it have a different scent, a different taste? How does it make you feel as it fills you?

 This energy is the embodiment of everything you have discovered about Water thus far in your study. It is cooling, and it is calm; it is powerful yet gentle in its movement. It is the distillation of perseverance. It is the flexibility to flow around the boulder in the stream, yet it is the endless patience to carve that boulder away into nothingness over the course of generations.

 Draw this energy into yourself and release it back into the place of Water with each breath.

 Become familiar with the sensations you experience when Connected to Water. Once you are sure you will remember them, you may release your Connection and find yourself back in your energetic Center.

 As in previous exercises, over the course of three breaths release the energy that you have stored in your Center and then return to normal breathing. When you feel that it is right for you to do so, open your eyes.

 Take the time to write about your experiences with this element in your journal.

AIR

Air is the third element on the Spectrum; less stable than Water, but not as volatile as Fire. Because of its intrinsic instability, it can be hard to work with Air. The danger here is not so much that it can overwhelm you and sweep you away as Water can, but that it is just difficult to maintain the connection. Unless you are paying close attention, your Connection with Air will let go and dissipate, and your work will be undone.

EXERCISE 10: Connecting to Air

As you proceed with this visualization, remember that it is yours to control and yours to end if, at any time, you feel yourself beginning to lose control of the flow of energy.

- *As when you prepare to Ground, place yourself in a comfortable position, close your eyes, and begin breathing deeply and regularly. Become aware of the flow of energy into and out of your body with each breath. As before, over the space of three breaths, take control of the flow of energy and separate that flow from the flow of Air into and out of your body. Collect the energy from three indrawn breaths in your Center and then return to the normal ebb and flow of energy as you continue breathing.*

- *Now form a picture in your mind of a place where there is a vastness of Air. You might see yourself standing beneath an endless sky, or you might envision flying as a bird through a place where there is no ground, only Air, up, down, and to each side.*

- *This Air is moving. There are breezes all around you. In the distance, you see a whirling column of it; not a tornado, but similar in shape. It is a vortex of purest Air, moving in circles and spirals but carrying no harmful debris. It is Air, no more and no less.*

- *Imagine yourself coming closer to this vortex. Move as close as you feel safe being. If you are truly adventurous, you might enter the vortex to feel its power. It cannot harm you; this is your archetype of Air, and it responds to your will.*

- *Once you have this visualization firmly in mind, reach out from your energetic Center and form a connection with the vortex. It does not matter what form this connection takes, as long as it is the connection that feels right to you. You might envision a tight tendril of rapidly-spinning Air that reaches out from the vortex and connects directly to your energetic Center. You might find yourself becoming as Air yourself, mingling with the vortex and dancing across in this place.*

- *Whatever way of connecting you wish to use, find it and know that the connection exists. Once you have done that, begin to draw energy across the connection. With each breath, take some of the energy of the Air into your Center.*

- *How is this energy different from the energy of Earth and Water? Is it warmer or cooler? Does it have a different scent, a different taste? How does it make you feel as it fills you?*

- *This energy is the embodiment of everything you have discovered about Air thus far in your study. It is invigorating, it is nimble; it is gentle in its movement, and swirls around you rather than forcing you in any direction. It is the distillation of whimsy. It is the ability to avoid a problem and to fly away to a new place.*

- *Draw this energy into yourself and release it back into the place of Air with each breath.*

- *Become familiar with the sensations you experience when Connected to Air. Once you are sure you will remember them, you may release your Connection and find yourself back in your energetic Center.*

- *As in previous exercises, over the course of three breaths release the energy that you have stored in your Center and then return to normal breathing. When you feel that it is right for you to do so, open your eyes.*

- *Take the time to write about your experiences with this element in your journal.*

FIRE

Fire is the most volatile of the physical elements. As I have stated before, in some ways it is not a physical element at all; it is instead the embodiment of transformation. For that reason, working with Fire is risky. It is the one physical element that will actively draw energy out of you across the Connection, if you allow it, because of its archetypal need for fuel to consume.

A word of warning: I strongly recommend that you do not attempt to make a Connection with Fire until you have practiced and mastered creating Connections with all of the other three physical elements. Even having mastered those, it is critical that you have a partner or spotter present with you when you try it, each and every time, until you have established a rapport with and an understanding of the Fire.

During the classes on this subject that I teach, different students display different reactions when Connecting to the various elements, but without exception, the most profound reactions occur during the Fire meditation. On more than one occasion, a student has required me to specifically call them out of the meditation. Proceed with caution: here there be dragons.

EXERCISE 11: Connecting to Fire

Remember, as you proceed with this visualization, that it is yours to control and yours to end if, at any time, you feel yourself beginning to lose control of the flow of energy. With this exercise in particular, if you feel yourself losing control, bring yourself out of it immediately.

- *As when you prepare to Ground, place yourself in a comfortable position, close your eyes, and begin breathing deeply and regularly. Become aware of the flow of energy into and out of your body with each breath. As before, over the space of three breaths, take control of the flow of energy and separate that flow from the flow of air into and out of your body. Collect the energy from three indrawn breaths in your Center, and then return to the normal ebb and flow of energy as you continue breathing.*

- *Now form a picture in your mind of a place where there is endless Fire. This is like no place on Earth; it is simply Fire, stretching out into the distance.*

- *This Fire is the essence of passion, of transformation. It never ceases movement, even for an instant. Do not allow yourself to lose focus while you are in this place, lest the Fire choose to consume you.*

- *Once you have this visualization firmly in mind, if you feel that it is safe for you to do so, reach out from your energetic Center and form a connection with the flames. It does not matter what form this connection takes, as long as it is the connection that feels right to you. Do not allow your concentration to lapse; Fire is not yet your friend, and you cannot yet trust it.*

- *Whatever way of connecting you wish to use, find it and know that the connection exists. Once you have done that, begin to draw energy across the connection. With each breath, take some of the energy of the Fire into yzur Center.*

- *How is this energy different from the energy of Earth, Water, and Air? Is it warmer or cooler? Does it have a different scent, a different taste? How does it make you feel as it fills you?*

- *This energy is the embodiment of everything you have discovered about Fire thus far in your study. It is passionate; it is certain of itself. It is that which consumes and transforms. It is the only element that cannot exist without something upon which to feed. It is the only element that cannot exist without change, for the Fire that is now is not the Fire that was but a moment ago. It is the essence of change. It is the ability to avoid or transform a problem or yourself; it is the ability to discover a way through where there was no way before.*

- *Draw this energy into yourself, and release it back into the place of Fire with each breath.*

- *Become familiar with the sensations you experience when Connected to Fire. Once you are sure you will remember them, you may release your Connection and find yourself back in your energetic Center.*

- *As in previous exercises, over the course of three breaths release the energy that you have stored in your Center and then return to normal breathing. When you feel that it is right for you to do so, open your eyes.*

- *Take the time to write about your experiences with this element in your journal.*

MAINTAINING AN ALL-DAY CONNECTION TO THESE ELEMENTS

We can maintain an all-day, every-day Connection to elemental Earth, but can we do that with the other elements?

Possibly. It would certainly be more difficult because of the less-stable nature of each. Certainly, it would require more conscious effort and be harder to leave in the realm of the subconscious, because the subconscious is not equipped to handle the shifting power of the less-stable elements.

Further, I actively recommend against trying it in the first place, because managing even a *little* instability all day long is going to cost you in terms of concentration as well as real, physical energy. Attempting to stay Connected to an element as ephemeral as Air or as aggressive as Fire would take nearly all of your concentration and would ultimately make it difficult for you to do anything but concentrate on your Connection.

To put it another way: you probably spend most of your day every day either sitting, standing, walking, or running, all on the stable surface of the earth or some other stable surface. Do you *really* have the energy to spend all of those same hours swimming? Or flying a hang-glider? Or walking on a bed of hot coals?

Even if you did have the energy, and you were to spend a whole day doing one of those things, how much else would you get done?

For that reason, stick to Earth for your constant, all-the-time Ground.

Is that all?

Students of mine often wonder: is the four-element model really complete? Does it really explain all of the phenomena that we can observe in the energetic realm?

No, actually, it is not complete. It's actually not even complete enough to explain all of the phenomena that we see in the physical realm.

Consider: From a physical, elemental standpoint, what is the difference in a body just before the moment of death, and just after? There is no difference that can be explained through physical means, yet the spark of life is gone—that tiny bit of the Divine that is often described as soul or spirit has departed.

There is no room on our planar model of the Elements for another one: on the one axis, we have Air and Earth in opposition to one another, and on the other axis, Water and Fire. To place an additional element on that diagram would be to break the model...

...unless we expand into the third dimension; we can place another axis orthogonal to the existing two, so that this new element, this life-giving force, this Animus, lies above the plane that is defined by the other four.

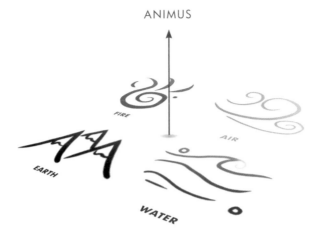

Now we have a model that contains all five of the elements for which we have observed a need. However, this model still has a flaw: it is out of balance. Air is balanced by Earth and Fire by Water, but there is nothing to balance Animus.

If Animus is the creative force, the source of vitality, then its balance must be the opposite: that which is the source of death, decay, and corruption. That which Animus would create, this balancing element would seek to annihilate. Thus, the name for this final element in our model: Nihilus.

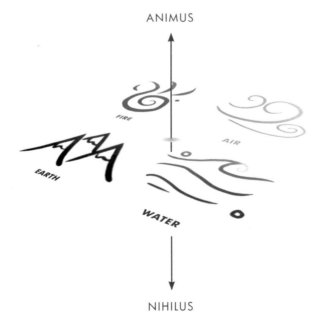

Neither Animus nor Nihilus is a physical element at all; they are things which exist solely within the realm of the spiritual, the energetic.

ANIMUS:

The Spirit of Creation

Many religions offer a story of creation. Before some moment, there was nothing, and after that moment, there was...everything. Even modern science with the Big Bang Theory contains this cusp of nothing-and-then-something and struggles to this day to explain from where all of that "something" came.

Animus, the creative force in our model, might then be likened to God the Creator, or the Source, the All, Mother Goddess, or the Great Spirit of the Universe, depending on your own particular spiritual or religious beliefs. It is the archetype of all creative energy, that which can produce something out of nothing.

NIHILUS:

The Spirit of Destruction

Few religions contain the idea of a universal destructive force—namely, destruction for the sake of destruction itself. Within Christianity, the force that is opposed to the God-Animus is the Devil, the Fallen One; destructive, certainly, but not in equal measure so as to counter the creative power of God. Within Hindu belief, Shiva perhaps comes closest, but he embodies both creation and destruction, and the destructive aspect of Shiva is not wanton, but is part of transformation.

True Nihilus has no motivation other than destruction, corruption, decay, and entropy. It cannot be reasoned with; it cannot be bought, bargained with, or bribed. It is antimatter to the matter of Animus. It is beyond the scope of thought.

CAN WE USE THESE TWO FINAL ELEMENTS IN OUR ENERGY WORK?

We have built archetypes of the physical elements, so as to visualize them and then establish an energetic Connection to each.

Could we do this with Animus and Nihilus as well?

Yes, we could. However, if you recall the Spectrum of Volatility with Earth on the stable end and Fire on the unstable end, consider that Animus would come to the right of Fire and Nihilus to the right even of *that*.

Historically, there have been people who have had religious experiences that leave them forever changed—unable to relate to the world as it is, seeking only the perfection that they once touched and cannot reach again. "God-touched," these people are sometimes called. Often they are viewed as insane. These may be people who have—through whatever means—touched Animus while being unprepared for it.

There have been other people in history who have been inexplicably evil; the breadth of their effect on the world is not as worthy of consideration here as the sheer focused destructiveness of will that they exhibited. Perhaps they were not so until they somehow opened a conduit between themselves and Nihilus.

I strongly recommend against even attempting to establish a Connection to either of these elemental archetypes. If you desire a connection with Animus, I suggest prayer and honest devotional work in whatever form your particular spiritual path provides. If you actually, truly desire a connection with Nihilus—wanton destruction with no purpose other than to destroy—go, right now, and seek professional help; there is nothing more that this book can do to help you.

Life in Balance

Within each relationship, the only one you have

control over is yourself.

In order to maintain each relationship

in balance, the only thing that you can

do is to change yourself.

APPLICATION TO THE REAL WORLD

Now we have completed our puzzle. We have, on the one hand, a well-practiced familiarity with the mechanics of controlling the flows of energy into and out of ourselves, and on the other hand, a solid understanding of the theory of archetypal elemental energy. Plus we have the piece that connects both of those: an experiential knowledge of how to pull energy of the various elemental types into ourselves.

Now all we need is something to do with all of that energy once we have it.

A WORD ON THE SUBJECT OF ETHICS

Before we leap into the practical application of everything that we have learned so far, it behooves us to take a moment to consider the critically-important difference between the words "could" and "should."

A formal exploration of ethics is, of course, beyond the scope of this book. There are varying schools of thought on even how to *define* right and wrong behavior before one even gets to the point of looking at different actions in terms of their ethical soundness.

Everything we have learned so far in this book can actually give us a fairly reasonable ethical compass upon which to proceed. The exercises related to Centering, Grounding, and Shielding are all expressions of individual will. *Your* individual will. You Center because it is no one's right but yours to define who you are. You Ground because it is no one's right but yours to move you from your stable place. You Shield because it is no one's right but yours to determine which energies reach you from the outside.

If we grant ourselves all of those rights, we in fairness must also grant those same rights to others, even if their ways, beliefs, and disciplines are different from ours. Even if they have not learned to Center, we have no right to attempt to change their sense of identity. Even if they have not learned to Ground, we have no right to try to force them from their stable place. Even if they have not learned to Shield, we have no right to force energy upon them that they do not wish to bear.

Consider this, always, when you are performing *any* kind of energy-work that will affect another: ask yourself, "Is what I am doing going to take freedom of will away from another person without that person's knowledge and consent?" If the answer to that question is anything other than an unequivocal "no," then you tread outside the bounds of ethical behavior.

That is a very black-and-white answer, and in the real world, there are very few things that are truly that clear-cut. There *are* circumstances when it is not only necessary but proper to act in a way that impedes the free will of another. Parents, for instance, are responsible for the well-being of their children and often have to make choices and take actions that go against what the children want. Defense of the innocent or helpless, against an aggressor, is another gray area that many people believe is justifiable.

Ultimately, you are going to act in the way that you are going to act. If you are *mindful* of what your actions mean and how they will affect other people, you are far less likely to take action that is unethical.

THE FIVE TYPES OF RELATIONSHIP

As part of the spiritual-education classes that we hold within our own religious community, my wife and I teach a segment on the subject of maintaining balance in one's relationships. Each and every one of us has many different relationships, which fall into one of five basic categories. Knowing which category a particular relationship falls into can give us guidelines as to how we must handle that relationship and on which aspects of that relationship it is important to focus.

Every relationship we have contains two energy flows: the outgoing one, leading from us to the other entity, and the incoming one, returning from the other entity to us. Together, the two entities and the two connections between them form a system. (Note that I do not say "people," because one of the entities may be something more abstract, like a company or a garden or Deity.) When the system is balanced, when each entity is giving and receiving in kind and the flows of energy along the connections are stable, the relationship itself is healthy. But when the flows are not balanced, when the give and take is going all in one direction, or when the energy that is flowing across a connection is of a detrimental kind, then the relationship falls out of balance.

When this occurs, it can create a feedback loop; for instance, if I treat my wife badly, that is energy of a detrimental type flowing along the connection from me to her. How she reacts to that treatment, to that energy, will ultimately affect the energy that returns to me along the other connection, the one from her to me. If she responds negatively, that's detrimental energy returning to me. I might be tempted to assume that the problem is hers; after all, I may not have even *noticed* myself treating her badly. If I do that—if I assume that she was the start of the issue (when in fact I was)—then nothing that I do thereafter will be able to re-balance the flows of energy between us.

For that reason, awareness of our *own* role in each and every one of our relationships is absolutely critical. If we can exercise enough self-awareness to know when we are sending detrimental or harmful energy out, we can make a conscious choice to stop doing so. If we are not yet capable of being self-aware to that extent but are willing to include ourselves in the list of suspects when a relationship begins to become unbalanced, we can at least take proper corrective action after the fact. If, in the above example, I notice hurtful energy coming across the connection from my wife and I do not jump to the conclusion that it's her fault but instead take a look at my own actions and at my outgoing flow of energy, I have a good chance of realizing that it was my initial bad treatment of her that led to the echo returning along the inbound connection.

You have already practiced performing a many-step energy-work process over and over until it becomes second nature and eventually becomes reflexive and subconscious. This process of paying attention to the outward- and inward-bound flows of energy for each of our relationships is no different: at first, you will have to be *consciously* mindful of the energy you are sending to others and of the energy you are receiving back from them.

Within each relationship, the only entity you have control over is yourself, so in order to maintain each relationship in balance, the only thing that you can do is to change yourself—to change the energy that you are sending out with the intention of rebalancing that relationship.

As you practice the conscious self-awareness of your actions, the energy you are putting into each relationship, and the energy you are receiving back, you will be training your subconscious mind to do the same thing. Over time, you will discover that you no longer have to pay active attention to how you are treating and being treated in your relationships; that monitoring will move to a subconscious level, and at that point, it will actually become very difficult for you to *have* an unbalanced relationship.

Once you reach that level of constant, subconscious, reflexive awareness of your role in all of your relationships, the final piece of the puzzle will fall into place: your subconscious will sense the type of elemental energy that is appropriate for each relationship in order to keep that relationship sound and balanced and will draw that energy into your center and send it across that outgoing relationship connection.

THE SELF

It may seem redundant to have an entire category of relationship for the Self. After all, we're not in a relationship with ourselves; we simply *are* ourselves, yes?

It turns out that the answer to that question is actually "no." The rational intellectual aspect of the mind is not always in accord with the emotional aspect of the mind and is not always in accord with the physical body. For that reason, we must treat the interaction between the intellect and each of these other aspects of Self as unique relationships, subject to the same rules of energy work as all other relationships.

THE EMOTIONAL SELF

The emotional self, the heart, is the part of us that does not *think*, but simply is. It is the place where our desires, our joys, and our sorrows are all rooted. We may know on an intellectual level that Grandfather is no longer in pain now that he has passed, but the emotional self is still sad that he is gone. We may know that a particular person is bad for us, but the emotional self may still yearn for him or her.

It is very important to maintain a balanced relationship between the intellect and the emotional self, because our emotions can easily either help or hinder us in our daily lives.

When the emotional self is dealing with a situation, it is up to the intellectual self to take a step back and determine whether the emotions are tending in a good direction or a bad one, and then, using the model of elemental energy, help to encourage the emotions if they're healthy or help correct or change them if they're unhealthy.

Example: *You are in a committed relationship with a wonderful life partner. An old partner from a former relationship shows back up in your life, and you find that, even though that person treated you very badly, you still feel lust or attraction for him or her and can't get it out of your head.*

In this situation, it's fairly obvious that the emotional self is attempting to lead you down a path that is unhealthy. So how can we use the elemental archetypes to deal with this situation? Lust and passion are within the realm of Fire. (You'll find that a lot of the motivations of the emotional self have a Fire energy about them.) In this particular case, each of the four elements offers a potential solution:

Earth is the embodiment of stability, of endurance, and of knowledge. In this situation, you know that your past with this person was harmful to you, and you know that your current partner is very good for you. Focusing on the stability of your current relationship and drawing the enduring Earth-energy into yourself can help you to remain strong and not to give in to the unhealthy passion.

Water is perseverance, a cooling influence, and the embodiment of thought. Draw into yourself the Water-energy and let it cool the heat of ill-placed lust. Actually think about what getting back into a relationship with that person would be like; remember the past, how he or she treated you, and think about whether that is something you want back in your life. Use that thought, as the Water shapes the stone, to build up the knowledge within you that you do not want that relationship back.

Air is avoidance and imagination. Draw the Air-energy into yourself and, when you begin to think of that person, let the Air of imagination pick up the Water of thought and carry it to a new place: perhaps let it fall as rain on the solid ground of the knowledge of how well your current partner treats you.

Fire is passion and transformation. You might "fight fire with fire," as the saying goes, by transforming any thoughts of passion you have for the former partner into thoughts of passion for your current partner.

Now that you are aware of how energy-work can affect the relationship you have with your emotional self, it's time to put that into practice.

EXERCISE 12: Affecting the emotional self

Take an introspective moment to consider your current emotional state. Find something within you that is an unhealthy emotion for you to be holding on to. Consider that emotion from the perspective of the elemental model and determine which element seems to represent it. Write as much as you can in your journal about what the emotion is, from where you think it may have come, and which element represents it.

> *Next, as in the example above, go through the physical elements and come up with a way that each of them might be used to help remedy the*

negative emotional state. It is sometimes difficult to find an idea for the element that is the same as the one that represents the harmful emotion. Try anyway, but if you cannot come up with one for that particular element, find at least one potential avenue for each of the other elements to help you. If you have more than one idea, that's great!

- *As you have each idea, write it down along with the element to which it corresponds. Practicing this exercise regularly will have two benefits. First, it will help you identify individual emotional states within you that are harmful to your own personal balance, and it will help you to identify ways of removing these emotional stumbling blocks. Second, you will grow accustomed to identifying the elemental associations of various emotions and of potential counters to those emotions, which will make it easier in the future to prevent those detrimental emotions from taking root in your mind.*

- *Every time you do this exercise, be sure to write about it in your journal; it will be a good record of the progress of your skill as well as your journey toward a balanced existence.*

THE PHYSICAL SELF

Do we even have an energetic relationship with our physical self? All of this "energy" that we are talking about is in the realm of the mind, not the body. So can this energy-work be used to affect the physical body as well?

Yes, it can. Physiologically, our minds and bodies are connected in such a way that our minds can *absolutely* affect our physical bodies. If you have any doubt of that, take a moment to think of a person you find to be very physically attractive. When you do that, your heart rate will elevate, your breathing will quicken, and you may notice other physical effects as well. All of those real, physical effects are brought about by a mere thought.

In energy-work, "as goes the mind, so goes the body." When we draw elemental energy into ourselves, the attributes of that energy are reflected into the way our physical bodies behave. Martial arts make frequent use of this phenomenon; a solid and forceful art like Tae Kwon Do makes much use of Earth energy to lend power and strength to kicks and punches and to give blocks the immobility of stone. A fluid art like Aikido is all about the Air energy: redirections, avoidances, and gentle pushes that toss an opponent as a tornado tosses everything in its path.

When we require a given physical effect, all we need to do is draw into ourselves the proper form of elemental energy:

- *Earth for strength, stability, immobility, endurance. Try having a friend push you off-balance. Then, draw Earth-energy into yourself and have them try again. You were far more stable and harder to unbalance the second time. Cats and children instinctively use Earth-energy when they don't want to be picked up.*

- *Water for perseverance, for flexibility, and for coolness. This is a great element to draw into yourself while you are exercising; it can help you to keep going when you feel as if you can't any more. Even better, the heat-dissipating properties of Water (the antithesis of Fire) can actually physically help to cool you when you are too warm. Try it on a hot day: draw elemental Water energy into yourself and feel your physical body dissipating some of the heat that you are feeling until you are more comfortable.*

- *Air for lightness and agility. When you need to be quick on your feet, nimble, able to dodge or dance or jump, draw the energy of elemental Air into you and feel your limbs become that much lighter and your spirits rise as they are lifted on the wind.*

- *Fire for passion and warmth. When you have a project that you want to be excited or enthusiastic about, draw elemental Fire into yourself and feel your passion for the project take on that heat. Your physical body will become more energized, and you'll be able to throw yourself into the task without hesitation. You can also use Fire for physical warmth. Try it on a cold day: open a Connection to Fire and let the heat of it suffuse your body. It will carry the chill away.*

EXERCISE 13: Applying energy to the physical body

- *Over the course of several days, try to identify various activities or situations where you could use the physical attributes of each of the four elements. Perform the Connection meditation for the proper element prior to undertaking these activities or entering these situations. Pay close attention to how your experience in those activities and situations is different from how it has been in the past when you experienced them without having reinforced yourself energetically first.*

▓ *After each, take the time to write about your experiences in your journal.*

▓ *Repeat this exercise regularly throughout the next several weeks; note how your ability to draw the elemental energy into you and use it on a situational basis becomes easier over time. If you continue to practice, this exercise will become second nature, and you will find that the energy stored in your Center will begin to shift reflexively in anticipation of your everyday situational needs.*

ENERGY AS A TOOL FOR SELF-AWARENESS

In fact, not only can we deliberately direct the energy to achieve some desired effect upon our physical bodies, but we can use the *undirected* flow of energy in order to explore our physical and emotional well-being and to discover things about ourselves that may require our attention.

Think back to the second exercise in this book: Centering. When you gathered energy via conscious energy breathing, it collected somewhere inside you. Where in particular it collected was not important for the purposes of that exercise, only the fact that it *did* collect. At that point in your journey toward control of the energy flows into, out of, and through you, you lacked familiarity with the process. Now that you have completed all of the previous exercises, the practice of consciously separating the flow of energy into you as you breathe will already be second nature. You no longer need concern yourself with whether the energy will gather, which frees you to explore in more detail an interesting question: Why does it gather where it gathers?

You may be familiar with a Japanese form of energy-work and healing known as Reiki, which was created (or perhaps discovered) by a Japanese Buddhist named Mikao Usui in the 1920s. Once trained and attuned by a Master/Teacher and thus able to administer Reiki treatments, a practitioner of this art is able to channel a type of universal healing energy into the recipient. While the details of Reiki and its practice are well beyond the scope of this book, one thing that is important to understand about Reiki is that the practitioner, while being a channel for the energy, *does not direct it*. The premise of Reiki, as originally described by Dr. Usui, is that the energy goes where it is needed, and it is the role of the one practicing Reiki only to provide a channel.

Whether the energy that we are discussing and using in our daily practice of Personal Energy Work is the *same* as the energy directed by an attuned practitioner of Reiki is probably a matter that one could debate at length. What is important is that, just as Reiki energy goes where it is needed, the energy that we draw into ourselves through conscious Energy Breathing, when left undirected, will do the same thing: it will collect within us in the place that it can do the most good.

That is why it is important for you to keep a journal of your daily practice with conscious Energy Breathing. By paying attention to where the energy collects within you, you can often become aware of needs that your physical or emotional self has before any other outward signs make themselves apparent. Your energy work will have a "default" place, where the energy collects under normal circumstances. It is not particularly important where that place is within you. What is important is that you note any *differences* in where the energy collects.

This is similar in concept to the baseline for vital signs that your doctor collects for you over time. Some people have blood pressure that is naturally a bit higher than average, and some naturally have a lower one. Once your doctor knows what your typical blood pressure is, he or she can then look for changes to that number, which may reflect a change in your health. Without such a baseline, a "normal" blood pressure reading would trigger no concern, but in a person whose pressure is usually lower than average, a "normal" reading could actually be several points elevated and therefore a problem in that particular person. Likewise, if your energy usually collects behind your Solar Plexus, but one day you begin to notice that it is collecting, for instance, farther up in your chest, it tells you something: it tells you that there is something going on with your physical or emotional self that has caused your energy-focus to move.

What that reason is will not always be obvious, but there are some clues to help determine how to proceed, once you note a difference. For instance, it is probably usual for the energy to collect in a place that is located along the center-line of your body, which leads from the top of your skull down to the base of your spine. If you suddenly note that the energy is collecting somewhere to one side or the other, especially if it is out in your extremities, that is a pretty good indication that your body is trying to heal itself of some damage or injury in that area.

You can pay attention to the physical location of various systems in your body and use that knowledge, along with your observations of where your energy collects, to discover areas of concern. If the cause for this shift in your energetic flow is not obvious—for instance, a recent injury or strain in that area—you might wish to speak to your doctor to rule out potentially-serious medical concerns.

When your energy-focus, your Center, moves within you but follows your center-line, it is possible that it may be moving in accord with your emotional or psychological needs rather than purely-physical ones. Those who follow the Hindu paths as well as some branches of Buddhism are familiar with the idea of Chakras. An in-depth discussion of the Chakra concept of personal energy flows is a topic for an entire book in and of itself. (In fact, there are several excellent books on the subject, and I recommend further study if what you learn in this brief overview resonates with you.)

In a nutshell, the Chakras are places within your body where the flows of energy intersect and collect. There are Chakras located throughout your body, but there are seven primary ones, which are located along a line that leads from the base of your spine up through the top of your head. Traditionally, the Chakras are counted from the bottom up, and each one is related to a particular aspect of your personality. When you find that your energetic Center has shifted to coincide with one of the seven Chakras, you might wish to explore the attributes of the emotional and psychological self that correspond to that Chakra.

The seven primary Chakras located within you are:

 ## The Root Chakra

This is located at the base of your spine, and it is primarily associated with the physical. Not the physical self but in how you relate to the physical world. When your energy suddenly begins collecting in your Root Chakra, it can be an indication that you do not feel secure in your life. Perhaps your home or job situation is not as stable as you would like it to be. Perhaps you do not feel sufficiently grounded or that you are being pushed around by the circumstances of your world. If you find that this is the case, you might choose to return to or increase your daily practice of Grounding in Elemental Earth. Doing so will provide you with the calm, stable energy you require in order to re-establish balance in the areas of your life that the Root Chakra governs.

 ## The Sacral Chakra

This is located a few inches above the Root in the area of your sexual organs and, appropriately enough, correlates strongly with the more primal urges and passions within us. Sex, certainly, but other generative aspects of ourselves are associated with this Chakra as well. A sudden shift of energy to your Sacral Chakra suggests that something is out of balance with your primal self, the part of you that does not think but simply is: your lusts, your passions, your creativities. The form of elemental energy you choose to apply to the situation will vary significantly, depending on your situation. For instance, if you reflect upon your emotional self and come to realize that your energy is directed at the Sacral Chakra because you are becoming more and more lustful toward someone that is unavailable (for whatever reason), the application of Fire energy would probably only make things worse! If the opposite case is true and you find yourself lacking creativity and passion in your life, some work with Fire energy may be exactly what you need. Meditate on *why* your energy is collecting in your Sacral Chakra and then evaluate as you did in earlier exercises what type of elemental energy can best help you correct any imbalance you find.

The Navel Chakra, *sometimes called the Solar Plexus Chakra.*

This is located in your core, a little above your navel and a little below your Solar Plexus, which is why it is referred to by both names. It correlates with the sense of self, and thus is often the "default" place where people collect energy during the Centering exercise. Recall that Centering is the act of stating "I am" to the universe, and there can hardly be an act more closely related to the sense of self. Since many people will naturally gravitate toward collecting energy in this place, it is sometimes the *lack* of energy collecting here that is significant. If you find that your energy collects in your Navel Chakra normally, and then suddenly you find that it does not collect there—and also does not move to a specific other location, thus indicating a problem there—but simply diffuses or will not collect at all, then you have a Navel Chakra issue to address. Problems of this sort often relate to a loss of sense of self or self-empowerment. Is something or someone undermining you at work or at home? Do you feel as if circumstance is requiring you to act in a way that you feel is not right for you? Once you have determined the underlying cause of this imbalance, you can determine which type of elemental energy to apply to the situation to bring it back on track.

 The Heart Chakra

This is, as you might expect, located in the center of your chest, where your heart resides. It is worth noting that many people are under the impression that the heart is on the left side of the chest; it is not. It is in the center behind the sternum, and only the lower tip of it projects to the left. The Heart Chakra resides in the same place and relates to emotion: both our own emotions and our connection to and understanding of the emotions of others. If you find that your energetic Center suddenly shifts to reside in your Heart Chakra, look to the emotional realm, both inward and outward, to discover the cause. Do you have some hurt that you bear within you and have not released and moved past? Is someone else, someone to whom you are connected, suffering from an emotional need? Emotion is often considered to be associated with elemental Water, except for those baser emotions that are more in keeping with Fire and the Sacral Chakra. Use this knowledge to explore possible elemental solutions to any imbalance you might find.

 The Throat Chakra

This is an energy focus located in more or less the same place as the larynx (the voice box). It governs communication as well as factual knowledge and understanding. A sudden shift of energy to the Throat Chakra could indicate that you are having difficulties in these realms. Perhaps you do not feel that your voice is being heard in a situation that is important to you? Perhaps something you have relied upon as firm knowledge in the past is no longer as sure to you, and you are troubled? Because fact and knowledge are very much Earth energies, you have a starting point from which to determine which type of energy you wish to apply to the situation to restore balance.

 The Third-Eye Chakra

Located upon the forehead or brow, this Chakra is most associated with seeing beyond the physical realm into the spiritual. When your energetic Center shifts to this place, it could mean that there is something going on in your spiritual life that requires your attention. Perhaps you have been ignoring the devotional aspect of your daily spiritual practice, and you need it more than you realize. Perhaps you are being led in a spiritual direction with which you have not yet come to terms, and you must reconcile it in order to proceed. This Chakra is more strongly associated with the spiritual element of Animus more than with any of the physical elements. However, you are a physical being as well as a spiritual one, and you can apply the energy of the correct physical element to your situation in order to allow yourself to progress.

 The Crown Chakra

This Chakra is sometimes described as being located on the top of the head and sometimes as being above the head, separated from the physical body by a few inches. It makes some sense that it would be separated from the physical, because it is our connection to the Divine. Not to the spiritual, which is our *understanding* of the Divine, but to the unfathomable concept of Divinity itself. This Chakra is entirely of the spiritual element Animus—or, in the case of some rare few, with its antithesis, Nihilus. Because the Crown Chakra is entirely of the spirit element Animus and of the Divine self that is separate from the physical, there is little influence the energies of the physical elements can have upon it. However, in all of my years of teaching, I have never had a student who found that their energetic Center moved all the way to the Crown; I theorize that this is because the Divine, by virtue of being Divine, does not become out of balance in the way that physical beings do, and since the Crown is our connection to that, it takes care of itself. However, should that theory prove to be false and you find that your energetic Center is drawn to your Crown Chakra, you have some work ahead of you; this could be an indication that there is some discord between you and the Divine itself. In this case, I recommend consulting with a religious leader in your community; someone in whom you have a good deal of trust and who can help you sort out what is going on.

As I stated prior, there are entire books related to the subject of the Chakras, and what I have covered here merely scratches the surface. Use this list as a guideline and allow your further research to help you refine your knowledge and understanding of the Chakras as you incorporate these concepts into your daily practice of Personal Energy Work.

Kin

When we talk of kin, for the purposes of this book, we can ignore the idea of blood-relationship and instead focus on the kinship of spirit that we feel with some people and do not feel with others. Genetic relationship is very much a matter of chance, and there is as much chance that you will feel no connection at all to a sibling, aunt, uncle, cousin, or other relative, as there is that you will feel a *definite* connection to someone who is no more genetically-related to you than to a stone.

When we speak of Kin relationships here, we are talking of the relationships that carry with them an emotional component: those people in whom we have placed some amount of trust. Close friends, partners, blood-relations we *are* close to...these are our Kin. Everyone else—whether they have a blood-tie to us or not—is relegated to the category of "Society."

Our interactions with Kin include many different levels of connection: the intellectual, the emotional, and (in many cases) the physical.

MATCHING ENERGY WITH WORD

Because we have a relationship with our Kin that carries emotional weight, the words that we say are a key part of the connection we have with those people. We discuss subjects with them that are close to our hearts or theirs—or both—and as a result, we must use care in the way we speak to them so as to ensure that the balance of the relationship is maintained. If you recall, back at the beginning of this book, I discussed the fact that ideas and words, as the conduit of those ideas, can possess the power to change the world. Words are a different type of the same energy that we have been manipulating throughout this entire study. Rather than being Divine energy that travels directly from the Center of one person to another, words take a detour through the intellect, twice, on the way from Center to Center. Twice, because they are filtered once through the intellect of the speaker and once again through the intellect of the listener.

As such, there is that much more potential for the flow to go awry. If, for instance, you wish to convey a bit of loving energy to your partner, there's the possibility that you might misspeak and say something other than what you mean. Likewise, there's the possibility that you will speak exactly what you mean, but your partner will hear incorrectly and the message still comes across garbled. Worst of all is the potential that you may misspeak and your partner may mishear, leading to a communication that is doubly wrong.

Unfortunately, we are fallible and mistake-prone beings, and there's no way to ensure that we will never say something in the wrong way, just as there is no way to ensure that the listener will always hear correctly.

There must be a way to minimize the negative impact of such miscommunications, and there is: through the use of the direct energetic connection you have with the other person. If, whenever you speak to one of your Kin, you reinforce what you are saying with energy of the same type, sent along the connection, then you have set up a kind of error-correcting mechanism. If either you misspeak or your partner mishears, and the words come across as negative while the energy that you have sent conveys a positive sentiment, at the very worst, your partner will notice a discrepancy between the two simultaneous messages and will probably ask you to clarify.

As an added benefit, if your words do come through clearly and the energy you send conveys the same sentiment, the message you are sending will carry twice the impact.

This works even with people who are not practiced in the areas of energy-work. As with all of the other techniques in this book, regular practice of this technique will lead to it becoming reflexive and subconscious.

MATCHING ENERGY WITH DEED

The saying "talk is cheap" is a simple way of expressing that if your words and actions do not match, it is the actions which are the better expression of your true nature. There is an energetic component to this truism as well: deeds with a particular intent that are backed by energy that mirrors that intent will seem that much more sincere, whereas deeds that conflict with the energy you are sending will seem false and contrived.

Additionally, if you perform an action that is easy to misinterpret, such as reaching toward someone's eye, but back it with the energy of your intention (e.g., you are trying to prevent a loose eyelash from falling into their eye and causing them discomfort), the other person will subconsciously respond to the hint that the energy gives them and be more open to your action.

EXERCISE 14: Energy-work with Kin

- *Take a moment to reflect, and find a person in your life who is important to you but with whom you seem to fail to communicate correctly.*

- *Using the technique of pushing energy that matches your words and deeds, get together with that person and have a conversation or perform some activity together (or, better still, do both). During the interaction, match your personal energy to the communication you are attempting to have and make note of whether the communication seems to be clearer when you are sending the matching energy along your connection to that person.*

Take a moment to write about this experience in your journal.

If you have more than one person in your Kin with whom you have unreliable communications, repeat this exercise with them as well. It may be necessary to repeat the exercise more than once with each person. Over time, you should see your relationships with each of these people improving, with fewer misunderstandings and an overall easing of tension between you. As this occurs, you will also notice that the energy you receive back on the connection from each person to you will become calmer and more appealing.

SOCIETY

This is the category for people with whom we have no particular emotional bond; they are people with whom we may or may not interact or may or may not even have emotional interactions (who hasn't gotten angry at a stranger on the road, after all), but who are outside of the sphere of those whom we specifically care about as individuals.

The people of Society are people with whom we have no particular emotional connection, so words are less critical as a means of energetic connection between us. The subjects that we talk about tend to be more superficial and, as such, are less likely to cut to the heart.

That is not to say that words spoken to someone we don't know or barely know cannot hurt. Some amount of mindfulness is still required when speaking to people in Society. For this purpose, no specific energy push is required for every interaction; rather, a general state of holding energy that is in tune with the personality one wishes to convey will prevent most potential for damaging speech, and basic etiquette will take care of the rest.

Since there are fewer avenues for energetic communication through words between us and members of Society, the focus of how people will perceive us is almost solely through our deeds. As described in the previous section, we can communicate quite a lot to strangers simply by ensuring that our personal energy signature is appropriate to the situation.

Example: This is a situation that actually occurred to me. I was in a grocery store several years ago. I was in an extreme hurry and in a bad mood as well. Everything inside me was Fire; there was anger and frustration bouncing around inside my head. Though I had no malice toward anyone in the store, I began to notice that people were looking at me with expressions that ranged from concern to outright fear, and some of them were actively turning around and leaving the aisle in which I happened to be.

- *The signature of Fire, which includes aggression—and even the potential for violence—coupled with the fact that I was wearing all-black clothes, a black leather biker jacket, and leather engineer boots, was communicating a message of danger to the others in the store.*

- *Once I noticed that I was inadvertently frightening people, I took a moment to re-Center myself, and then I Grounded and pushed all of that anger and frustration into the Earth. Then, I drew the calm, stable, non-aggressive Earth energy back into myself and returned to shopping.*

- *As if I had flicked a switch, people stopped looking at me as if I were likely to pull a knife. Suddenly, I was just another shopper in the store, yet I was still wearing exactly the same clothes, the same jacket, and the same boots. By replacing all of that aggressive Fire energy with calm, non-aggressive Earth energy, I was able to transform my own demeanor as well as people's perceptions of me.*

By consciously deciding what energetic signature we should be projecting to the people around us and then drawing the corresponding elemental energy into our Centers, we can rapidly adjust to any given public situation.

Draw Earth energy when you need to convey calm, strength, or steadfastness. Draw Water when your need is to express gentle caring or a willingness to support someone. Draw Air when whimsy, lightheartedness, and imaginativeness are appropriate. And draw Fire during the times when you must appear passionate or even aggressive.

EXERCISE 15: Using elemental energy to change our aspect in public

- *Go to a public place where there are lots of people. A shopping mall or popular park is a good place to do this, but make sure it's a place where you're allowed to spend a good amount of time without getting in trouble for loitering. Spend some time simply observing people's reactions to you as you move through the place. Take a moment to stop and write down your impressions of how people are acting toward you in your Journal.*

- *Then, perform the Grounding exercise and fill your energetic Center with Earth energy. Once you have done this, spend more time interacting with people and see if you notice any difference in their reaction to you. It's entirely possible that the change will be minimal or non-existent, especially if by this time you have reached the point in your practice where you maintain a Ground connection more or less constantly. Regardless of how much or how little difference you notice, write what you observe in your journal.*

- *Once you have done that, perform the Connection exercise for Water and draw the energy of that element into your Center. Once more, move about and observe people's interactions with you while you are flooded with the energy of Water. Write down your observations.*

Repeat the process with Air and finally with Fire.

- *Once you are done, take the time to go over what you have written and see if you notice any patterns in the changes you observed in people's behavior. If you noticed no difference between your "default" self and when you deliberately Grounded in Earth, congratulations, that's actually a very good sign! It means that your practice of maintaining a Ground*

connection at all times is working and that you have the stable demeanor
and unthreatening aspect of Earth energy present without having to try.

- *What ways did people react to you when you were Connected to Water,*
  Air, or Fire? What can you take away from this? Pay close attention to
  the types of reactions you received because there may be a time when
  you want people to react to you in a particular way, and one method of
  accomplishing that would be to draw the type of elemental energy that
  led them to react that way in the past.

NATURE

Our relationship with Nature is not like other relationships, because Nature is not a
person—which is not to say that Nature does not have a personality; you will likely notice
several *different* personalities as you interact with various parts of the natural world.

All of those physical parts of the world that we live in, other than the people of Kin and
Society, fall into the category of Nature relationships. The relationship you have with
the dog across the street, with the trees in your yard (if you're lucky enough to have

some), or with the hornets whose nest you've inadvertently walked close to, these are all relationships with some aspect of Nature.

Example: Your relationship with a neighbor's aggressive dog

- *Dogs live in a simpler world than we do; theirs is a hierarchy of dominance and submission and of an even more clearly-defined map of Kin and not-Kin than we as humans possess. A dog that is showing aggressive behavior is doing one of two things: it is attempting to establish a hierarchical relationship to determine which of you will be the dominant one, or it is attempting to defend those it considers Kin from you, someone it considers to be not-Kin.*

- *You may have heard the old truism that a dog can smell fear. In a sense, that is true. But what is really happening is that a dog, like most animals, is very much attuned to the flows of energy around it and can sense the energy of fear (or lack of it).*

- *Aggression born of a desire for dominance is a type of energy that falls within the category of Fire energy. Because fear is Fire-type energy as well, meeting aggression with fear simply causes the Fire aspect of the interaction to become unbalanced, and that can lead the dog to attack you. In such a case, a better element to make use of might be Water or Earth, the cooler, more stable elements; a person connected to Earth or Water is not fearful and is not aggressive but at the same time shows no weakness. By displaying this sort of energy to the dog, you will be de-escalating the situation by indicating that you are not afraid and not submissive, while at the same time not a threat.*

- *If the dog appears to be defending its home or Kin, that is also a very Fire-based sort of energy, but it carries with it the immobility and unwillingness to compromise that is inherent to Earth. In this case, the energies of Water and Air might be useful to you; Water, again for the cooling calmness, and Air for its intrinsic tendency to avoid conflict: if you are no longer seeking to approach the boundaries the dog has established and go around them instead, the dog will have no reason to feel its Kin are threatened and will likely stand down.*

Dogs are a relatively common kind of Natural interaction, and most of us have had to cope with an aggressive dog at one point or other. The suggestions outlined in the example are no different from advice you may have received in the past with regard to how to deal with such a situation but are presented here primarily to show you how the things you already *know* and have seen at work fit into this elemental framework of relationship and, therefore, how when you expand your understanding of how to use the framework, the energetic interactions you have will be similarly successful.

Another type of Nature interaction, and one that may seem not as straightforward to resolve, is a run-in with a hive.

Example: your relationship with a disturbed hive

- *It is not wise to disturb the home of a hive of bees, wasps, or hornets. Those three types of stinging insects vary in intrinsic aggressiveness from least to greatest in the order that I have listed them. Bees, including honeybees, bumblebees, and carpenter bees, are all relatively complacent and will not initiate conflict. Wasps are very much more watchful and will harass anyone or anything that comes too close to their nest. Hornets, the most aggressive of the lot, will defend their hive from even a cursory threat and will start trouble at the least provocation.*

- *You might notice that this scale of relative aggression mirrors the Spectrum of Volatility described earlier in the book. Bees fall nearer the Earth end, and it should therefore be no surprise that they have other attributes associated with homey Earth activities: gathering and storing food, and so on; whereas the more aggressive wasps and hornets hunt and kill their food, a very much more Fire-aligned temperament.*

- *When you find yourself having to deal with one or more members of a Hive, you can make use of this knowledge to guide your actions.*

- *In all cases, Water is a helpful element to draw. Its calming influence will not disturb the gentler bees, and it will not be taken as aggressive by the more belligerent wasps and hornets. Air, of course, and its intrinsic tendency toward avoiding situations altogether is an effective strategy if it's applicable.*

- *Unfortunately, with highly-aggressive hives like yellow jackets and other ground-hornets, the only option ultimately may be to use the aggressive aspect reflected by elemental Fire: to destroy the nest before it can damage those who are innocent. (Note, this is not a suggestion that one use physical fire to destroy a nest; the risks inherent to such a plan are too great. Here we are talking about the aggressive aspect of Fire guiding our actions, but a more mundane means of carrying those actions out.)*

Beyond such relatively small and particular interactions you experience every day, the relationship you have with the cyclical passing of the seasons is a form of interaction with Nature. It is, perhaps, even more important than the everyday interactions.

In our daily lives, modern conveniences such as air conditioning, machinery, and relatively-simple travel from one part of the world to another have caused us as individuals to become far less tightly-connected to the ebb and flow of energy that occurs in the world itself with the changing of the seasons. Where once winter was a time for quiet domestic activities, community cooking, and introspection because snowfall limited travel, growing cycles limited food availability, and the sun's cycle shortened the useful hours of daylight, in the modern world winter is mostly seen as an inconvenience punctuated by occasional opportunities for snow-related fun. Plows clear the roads that once would have been impassable for days or weeks, trucks and airplanes bring summer fruits and vegetables to the grocery stores, and electric power grants us the opportunity for sun-bright light even in the darkest winter.

Likewise, summer's activities were limited by heat and by the need to take advantage of the growing season to work in the fields to store food for later. However, we can now undertake the most strenuous of activities on the hottest days of the summer, cool in the comfort of an air-conditioned arena. For most of us, food production is something that is handled by a faceless "someone else."

Through all of this, we have allowed ourselves to become disconnected from this natural cycle, but it is a *false* disconnection, for our bodies are still physiologically connected to the passing of the seasons. Ironically, when we find evidence of our bodies following the natural patterns, we label it a disease and take action to medicate it away. Two hundred years ago, everyone shifted activities in the wintertime, becoming less outgoing and focusing inward. They slept more and moved less as a way of conserving energy since food was limited. This reduction in activity was brought on by the changing cycle of sunlight; as the days dimmed, people nested for the winter.

Today, on the other hand, if a person is not as vivacious and engaged in activities in winter as he or she is in summer, we label it Seasonal Affective Disorder, and we put that person on medication designed to bring that person back up to so-called "normal" levels of activity.

Consider that for a moment: As a society, we are using drugs to force people to become less connected to the natural flow of the seasons in order to make them conform more completely to an *artificial* pattern of behavior.

EXERCISE 16: Recognizing the elements in the cycle of the year

- *Spend some time in meditation upon the passing of the seasons. Try to focus not on what human activities are going on in the world but what activities the natural world is undertaking in order to adjust to the changes in weather, light, and temperature. What do the trees do in each of the seasons? What do the other animals do? What does the world itself do, in your region, with each season's arrival?*

- *Write all of these observations down in your journal, then, using what you have come to understand of the elemental model of the world, consider which of the four physical elements might best be associated with each of the four seasons. Consider not only the physical aspects of each season such as temperature but also the types of natural activities that occur during these times. Write down your ideas regarding the elemental/ seasonal associations. There is no right or wrong answer in this activity, and if you happen to compare notes with someone else who is doing the same thing, do not feel discouraged if your associations and theirs are not the same.*

- *By establishing these associations in your mind, you are creating a model for yourself that will allow you to guide your own deliberate energetic activities in order to maintain a more-balanced interaction with the world as the seasons pass through their cycle.*

- *You may wish to align your energy with the energy of the season as you perceive it so that you can "go with the flow," as it were. On the other hand, need may cause you to Connect to a different kind of energy from the one prevailing in the season in order to help yourself cope with a difficult situation or circumstance presented to you by the natural world.*

- *As you practice all of this, keep notes in your journal tracking your progress.*

THE DIVINE

We have already discussed the premise that individual people each carry within them a bit of the Divine. As such, one might say that our relationship with Self is a relationship with the Divine. That is true to an extent. However, for the purposes of clarity, in this section we refer to that which is both Divine and outside of the Self.

If one records all of the metrics of weather in a given region over a significant length of time—decades or longer—one can begin to understand the *climate* of that region. In that way, "weather" is just a single point of data, whereas "climate" is the aggregation of thousands or millions of such points.

Likewise, the bit of divinity that is carried within each person is a single spark, but "The Divine" is the aggregation of millions or billions of those sparks as well as that which is divine but is not within any given person. The Divine is a motivating force in history as well as in the development of life itself. It is far larger and more powerful than any one person, any one community, any one country, or perhaps even any one world.

As such, having a relationship with such an immense thing might seem ridiculous to contemplate. It could seem as silly as one of the cells in our body sending us an e-mail, asking us to be friends.

However, it is not as absurd as we might think: Consider that, while cells within our body are born and die and are replaced on a daily basis and we are not even aware of the process, that process is nonetheless *vital* to our continued existence and, when it goes awry, can threaten our very survival. Everything in the body—from the creation of new life to the devastation of cancer—begins with a single cell.

For a child to progress from a fertilized egg to a fully-realized and independent human, that single cell must be supported as it divides over and over, achieving and fulfilling the potential outlined in its genetic code. If it is *not* supported, it may never divide even that first time. If the support falters during its growth, it may not survive or it may not develop properly.

On the other hand, for a cancer to progress from a single aberrant cell into a body-killing tumor, the immune system of the body must not have noticed it when it was weak enough to extinguish.

As the body is a collection of cells that must be supported and nurtured (or, alternatively, singled out and destroyed before they cause harm), so is the collective Divine the sum of the individual divine beings in the universe, who must be supported and nurtured if they are to thrive and fulfill their potential (or, as a cell that is on the verge of becoming cancerous, prevented from twisting in a harmful direction).

So it is not only *possible* for us to maintain a relationship with the greater Divine, it is critical that we do so: first, because if we are on a beneficial path with our life, so that we can be nurtured and supported on that path; and second, because if we are on a path that leads in a harmful direction, we will be open to receiving the lessons and guidance that will help redirect us into a healthier course of action.

It has been my experience that the Divine speaks to us through lessons that progress from gentle to forceful. This is not unlike when we drive on a highway: as long as we are staying in the proper lane, the way is smooth, but if we are not paying attention and begin to drift toward the verge, our tires hit the rumble strips to let us know that we are straying. If we take the hint and get back on the road, that's the end of it. If, however, we ignore the rumble strips, we may end up on the even-rougher shoulder and then off the road completely. If we still do not correct ourselves, eventually we will crash.

If the initial lessons of the Divine are not noticed, they become more forceful so that they cannot be missed. If they are actively ignored, then eventually they may lead to a crisis where all of our forward progress stops because we were headed in a direction that could have led to severe harm to ourselves or others. When we meet such a crisis, such a "teaching moment," we have the opportunity to regroup, to determine *where* we went off track, and how not to do it again. It may take us quite a long time to recover from such an event, however, so it is better to avoid getting into that situation in the first place.

The key lies in becoming attuned to the smaller lessons (the "rumble strips") so that we can redirect ourselves *before* we run off the road.

In order to do this, we must pay attention to our relationship with the Divine, just as if it were another person. There are two energy flows within this relationship: one is the flow from us to the Divine, outgoing, and the other is the flow from the Divine to us, incoming.

The one thing that makes this relationship unique among all of our relationships is that *everything we do, regardless of whether it affects anyone else, echoes along our outgoing connection to the Divine.*

Think about that for a moment: we hold within us a spark of the Divine, as does each person. Because that spark is the little bit of energy that defines us as a living, aware being, it's inescapable that everything we do as an aware being affects that spark. As that spark is part of the greater Divine, we cannot avoid the conclusion that everything we do *affects the greater Divine.*

Depending on your own personal theology, that may be a comforting thought or an exceptionally unnerving one. Regardless of how you think of it, it is nonetheless the case, so it is something that we must deal with rather than overlook.

The downside of this is that nothing negative we do can be hidden from the Divine. The upside is that, at this point in our practice of Personal Energy Work, we have taken conscious control of how we interact with ourselves, our Kin, the people of Society, and even Nature itself. Because we have taken those interactions under conscious control, we are far less likely to be acting in a negative manner. As mature beings, we do not *choose* to be harmful or negative as a matter of course. As our other four types of relationships move toward mindful balance, our relationship with the greater Divine will follow suit almost automatically.

In a sense, awareness of the ebb and flow of energy in all of our various relationships is awareness of our relationship with the Divine. However, it can be an overwhelming thought to consider each and every one of our relationships, in turn, checking each for imbalance as a way of checking in on our relationship with the Divine. So it would be handy to have a shortcut, of sorts: a quick way to survey our overall energetic relationship with the Divine and to see if there are areas that are conspicuously out of balance so that we might then address them.

EXERCISE 17: Conscious awareness of the relationship with the Divine

- *You may perform this exercise either as a meditation or as a simple time of quiet introspection.*

- *Take the time to consider the things that have gone on in your life over the past several days. It's likely that some things will have gone better than others. Pay attention to each of the areas of relationship (not the relationships themselves) and make note of any common themes that you have had to address in all of them. For instance, pay attention if several people have been impatient with you or angry at you, or if you have had difficulty with time management on several occasions. Once you have identified the various places where you have had difficulties, focus on the elemental influences that seem to be behind those difficulties. Using what you have learned so far, classify each type of difficulty as an imbalance of one or more types of elemental energy. If you identify any areas where there seems to be a common influence, then you can further determine which elemental influences you can draw upon to balance yourself, so that those relationships are no longer out of balance. For instance, your relationships with Kin and Society all seem to be centered around an excess of Fire energy that is causing you to act in a way that is more generally aggressive than is productive. Use your knowledge about the different elemental influences to determine how best to alter the situation to benefit everyone.*

- *If, on the other hand, it seems that relationships in one direction seem to be troubled by one type of elemental imbalance and relationships in another seem to be governed by a different type, that is an indication that you may be pulling energy from one relationship area to put into another. That means that the type of relationship that is taking excess energy is causing you to pull from your other relationships, rather than pulling the required energy from your Ground or other Connection.*

- *Centering, Grounding, and Shielding. If you have need of a particular type of elemental energy to deal with the current imbalance, Connect to the element and use its energy to do what is required.*

- *Once you are done with this exercise, write about your experience in your journal.*

◼ *Repeat this exercise approximately once a week, so that you have a regular record of your overall state of balance.*

Pulling energy form one relationship to serve another is ultimately fruitless, because it is, as the saying goes, "Robbing Peter to pay Paul." You are taking energy that, after a fashion, *belongs* in one place, and putting it in another place. That will ultimately create an imbalance in the relationship type from where you are taking energy, which might require that you take more energy from yet another place. That is the beginning of a spiral that is very easy to let out of control.

Returning to the basics of energy breathing, Centering, Grounding, and Shielding gives you the opportunity to start over with a clean slate and may additionally help by reinforcing your shields. It's possible, after all, that the reason you became unbalanced in the first place is because you were allowing your shields to waver, which began allowing external influences to guide your allocation of energy rather than you guiding that allocation with conscious will.

RELATIONSHIPS THAT CANNOT BE BALANCED

Up until now, we have talked only in terms of taking whatever action is necessary to balance the flows of energy in your relationships. Does that mean that, no matter how badly a relationship is going, it is possible to correct it using these energy-work techniques?

Unfortunately, no, that isn't the case. There are relationships that either simply cannot be fixed, or they *could* be fixed, but at such great cost that they might as well be unfixable. A key indicator of a relationship that is unfixable is one where the energy flow along the "return" path from the other person to you never varies, or varies in a way that is not affected by the energy that you send out along the outgoing connection. When you are in a relationship of this type, there is no reciprocity and no give-and-take, so you have no way of balancing what you send and what comes back. If the energy that you are receiving back from such a person is energy that is detrimental or harmful to your balance, you have little choice but to sever the relationship in order to protect yourself and, perhaps more importantly, those who rely on you to keep them from harm.

Another indicator is a relationship where, no matter how much energy you put into it, it never seems to be "enough." This is the symptom of a person who has no energetic Center or no awareness of one, who therefore casts about a Grounding connection at anyone who will let them. If you allow such a person to use you as their Ground, they will take from you and take from you, until there is nothing left. It might be possible to feed them the energy that you can pull across *your* Ground, but that is an example of giving a man a fish rather than teaching him to fish. You would spend all day every day thereafter managing your energy flow solely for the benefit of another, which is a disservice to yourself as well as to all of your other relationships.

In this latter case, it's possible that the person can learn to manage their own energy flows. If they seem receptive to the idea, give them this book and allow them to decide whether they will stand up before the Divine and declare, "I *am* responsible for my own self." If they do not—or will not—then they are not your responsibility to continue to feed.

In Conclusion

We have learned to declare our
unique and enduring presence and
identity to the greater Universe.

As we have journeyed through the different sections of this book, we have explored several areas of personal awareness that may have been new to you or that you might have been aware of but had no way of explaining.

We have learned to declare our unique and enduring presence and identity to the greater Universe. We have learned to connect ourselves to a stable place so that we can exist within a realm of energy flows that are greater than we are. And we have discovered how to create for ourselves a sheltered place in these flows where nothing can reach us but those things we specifically choose to allow.

We have practiced the techniques for doing all of these until they have become second nature, reflex, and subconscious habit.

We have studied the archetypal alchemical elements of old, exploring how they apply to the physical world around us and, more importantly, to the world of energetic flows within us. We have experienced each of the physical elements and written down what we have learned about them, as a way of broadening our understanding of their physical attributes and therefore the attributes that they carry, as archetypes, into the realm of the mind.

We have considered several different ways of using these elemental archetypes to affect the flows of energy within ourselves.

We have forged connections with each of the physical elements and drawn their energy into ourselves; we have experienced the differences in sensation and effect that each of them has upon us.

We have discussed how all of this energy work, this conscious control over the flows of energy into and out of each of us can be used to deliberately alter the relationships we have with ourselves, our Kin, Society as a whole, the world of Nature that surrounds us, and with the very Divine itself. Using this knowledge, we have learned how to maintain balance in ourselves and in all of our relationships.

We have thought about how we can use all of this new-found knowledge to affect other people and when it is right or wrong to do so.

I say "we," but what I mean is "you." *You* have done all of these things. Each and every one of the techniques in this book is now yours to practice, and expand upon, and refine, until you have created your own unique approach to energy work so that you can create for yourself that thing we set out together to create:

A life in balance.

PHOTO CREDITS: